FINDING YOUR SUPERPOWERS IN THE PLACE YOU LEFT THEM

Finding Your Superpowers in the Place you Left Them

Sean "Bear" Bailey

Bear and Bailey Productions

Contents

Notes

When I first started down this journey, the world had not been turned on its head as it is now. 2020 highlighted another murder of a black man by police officers, along with several other senseless killings, beatings, harassment, and incarceration. We witnessed the continued injustices against people of color, which has only brought the spotlight back to the inequalities, racial profiling, and police brutality Americans live with daily. We are in the midst of a pandemic that has killed 100s of thousands of Americans and counting. We are experiencing the stoking flames of a race war that really never quelled fueled by our 45th President, his supporters, and those that believe in white supremacy. We keep meeting many Karens as they are now exposed and out in the open more than ever. And we feel the pain of millions of Americans who file for unemployment, lose their homes and shut down their businesses, identify, and livelihood.

As a black man, I feel rage, anger, stress, depression, and disappointment. So I get involved. I peacefully protest injustice and police brutality. I speak my truth to a group of strangers. I encourage others in the fight to keep the spotlight on the issues and warn against getting distracted. So here we are. The fight continues. The powers in play are strong, but we have a voice. I encourage everyone to use that voice. Now is not the time to be silent. Now is not the time to wish for normal. Now is not the time to wait for tomorrow. Now is exactly what it should be. Now!

Keep fighting a good fight, or as the late great John Lewis would say, "Good trouble." (Rest in Power)

Breonna Taylor, Ahmaud Arbery, Police Captain David Dorn, Rashard Brooks, Daniel Prude, George Floyd, Atatiana Jefferson, Aura Rosser, Stephon Clark, Botham Jean, Philando Castille, Alton Sterling, Michelle Cusseaux, Freddie Gray, Janisha Fonville, Eric Garner, Akai Gurley, Gabriella Navarez, Tamir Rice, Michael Brown, Tanisha Anderson, and all the countless others whose lives didn't need to end senselessly. We miss everything that you would have become!

Acknowledgements

Finding the knowledge, courage, will, and silence to writing a book is harder than I thought. There were so many moments of excitement followed by disinterest and doubt. Teetering back and forth became a constant. Finding other things to do was my vice until the silence in my head became too loud to put this off any longer. None of this would have been possible without the support and encouragement of my partner in life, Jonelle. From reading early drafts to giving me advice on the cover to keeping me hydrated with tea and water. You are so important to this book getting done as I was. Thank you so much!

To the team at Bear and Bailey Productions who enables me to be part of a family dynamic that keeps me enlightened and spiritually grounded. It is because of your smiling faces, efforts, and encouragement that I have a legacy to pass on to my family where one didn't exist before. Thank you so much Joshua and Olivia for showing up every day.

Although this period of my life is still unfolding as I continue to explore the truths inside of me, I am certain that every person that I have encountered taught me something; good or bad. From my third grade teacher, Ms. Baker, to my childhood friends, Chris and Ronnie in Brooklyn to my crew in college in VA, Tom, Al, Joe, Cedric, Ike, Duane and Rob to the boss who said my work wasn't good enough. I am thankful for all of it.

I've learned that everything has its own life force, its own spirit. Having a spirit of gratitude is how I choose to live, so thank you to every person, friend, foe, and everything in between for the impression you have made in me on this journey.

Finding Your Superpowers in the Place you Left Them
By Dr Sean "BEAR" Bailey

"Why would I want you to think like me. I'd rather help you learn how to think for yourself so that you can control your own narrative." - Me

For the Reader

Start with the Conclusion

HINT: start this journey by reading the conclusion at the end of the book and then come back to the introduction

Definitions

hu·man·i·ty

.. ..
.. ..

/(h)yoʔoˈmanƏdē/

1. human beings collectively, the fact or condition of being human.
2. the quality of being humane; benevolence.
3. learning concerned with human culture, especially literature, history, art, music, and philosophy.

re·la·tion·ship

.. ..
.. ..

/rəˈlāSH(ə)n͵SHip/

1. the way in which two or more concepts, objects, or people are connected, or the state of being connected.
2. the way in which two or more people or groups regard and behave toward each other.
3. the state of being connected.

su·per·pow·er

.. ..
.. ..

/ˈsoʔopƏr͵pou(ə)r/

1. a very powerful and influential force.

Introduction: My Story

"I learned to ask questions and demanded my father show me things that mattered to me."

It's my sophomore year in college, and I'm sitting in an auditorium waiting for my 10 am humanities class to begin. There were at least 150 students in this lecture, and we were all trying our hardest to pay attention to the facilitator. On the other side of the desk, Professor McManus was working just as hard to teach the class as we were trying to pay attention to it. Maybe it was the size of the audience or that the content didn't allow for much interaction, but I couldn't imagine having to stand up in front of this class and deliver a lecture day after day.

Nonetheless, the professor was very animated. He would use body gyrations, wave his hands about, and get on his knees now and then. I also recall him standing on a trash can at one point during the semester. I thought he was just losing it and did all of this just to entertain himself and get through the day.

For someone that suffers from acute attention deficit hyper disorder (ADHD), you can imagine how relieved I was to have this level of entertainment at my disposal. I was also a student-athlete, so I was always thinking about practice, weight training, eating, training some more, eating, another practice, study hall, and eating some more. As fascinated as I was with the professor's performance, I quickly lost sight of what I was supposed to be learning. I could remember him waving his hands, shouting certain words in the air, and a rhythmic tap of the toes, but the lesson not so much! As I mentioned, it was a humanities class, and that's all I remember for sure. So why was I there? What was I supposed to be able to do after taking the course? If I couldn't remember anything but the professor's mannerisms, how would I pass the test?

Frustrated with what I was feeling and anxious about the probability of not passing the test, failing the course, and getting in trouble with my coach, I went to see Professor McManus during his office hours. As I approached his office, I could hear music playing from behind the door. It was some sort of funky rock jazz type of music, but I couldn't make out the words because it was in a foreign language. I knocked on the door, entered the office, and expressed my concerns about what I was or wasn't learning from class. I also elaborated on the consequences of failing the course for me as a student-athlete, which would usually get me the results I desired (it worked with mostly every other professor).

He said to me, eyes peering over his glasses and almost looking past me, "*What is it that you want to learn?*"

Puzzled by his question, I responded, "*How am I supposed to know? You're the professor. I'm here to learn whatever it is you're supposed to teach me.*"

He replied, "*Is that my job? To teach you what you don't know or to show you how to learn so that you can teach yourself?*" At that moment, I recalled my level of confusion and saying to myself, "*What in the world does that mean?*" However, my aggravation got the better of me and prevented me from finding the right words to express my level of frustration without going full Rambo (***Rambo I*** not II, III, IV, or V).

He began to tell me about his background and why he became a teacher in primary school and later a professor. He mentioned how getting an education as a poor, Jewish boy in Brooklyn was a struggle. He spent a lot of time working in his father's shop and found that he learned so many more life lessons here than his dull classroom experience. In class, he couldn't pay attention, he didn't care about what the teachers were saying, and he lost interest in formal structured learning. But for some reason, the lessons he learned in the shop carried over to the classroom, and he found himself doing quite well in school despite his lack of enthusiasm and even less interest from his teachers.

"What was the key? What was the point of him telling me this?" I asked myself.

The professor's next line would clear this up for me, as he stated, "*I learned to ask questions and demanded my father show me things that mattered to me.*" Not only that, but he also said that his father challenged him to think for himself and encouraged him to push past his comfort zone. As a result, he didn't want other kids to miss out on this life lesson, so when he got old enough, he started to teach in a way that reminded him of his father.

When I left his office, I began to realize that my professor was intentionally making us uncomfortable by not knowing what we were supposed to be learning. He wanted us to do what I just did: ask questions and demand to learn what mattered most to us. He wasn't just going through the motions. He was offering us the opportunity to teach ourselves, think for ourselves, and be the owners of our learning journey. I took that lesson into every class going forward. I took that perspective into every video session, every practice, and every workshop or seminar. I applied this thinking as I moved into my residencies, into my 1-2-1 with my bosses, and into my organization with my staff. Now, I'm infusing it into this book, as you will soon see.

HOW THIS BOOK
WILL BENEFIT YOU

So let's be clear: this is by no means a self-help book. I won't pretend that I've figured everything out and that I don't still struggle with anxiety, depression, insecurities, stress, and some form of addiction. It's cathartic to share the stories and experiences that I have had. It's my way of kicking my demons in the ass and allowing my vulnerabilities to take centre stage. In other words, I needed to put a soul in this book, which comes from a deep place that most of us are hesitant to have others see.

This is NOT a book based solely on the profession of Learning and Development or Training. No one wants another *"How to"* book in training practices!

Yes, this is my chosen profession in which I am passionate about. Helping others to think and be the best version of themselves is my Superpower. It's what I do! The Learning and Development discipline is what I've researched and studied. I have learned from the most talented minds, and I've embraced my responsibility to influence others' lives in a positive way. This book is focused on how we can use our humanity and knowledge to become more self-aware to impact the very thing that we're all uniquely passionate about. We all have different walks. In my case, it happens to be the goal of inspiring people and organizations to think, to demand and expect more of themselves, and to encourage a willingness to have a mindset of lifelong learning. Insert [*your passion here*] and take the stories shared as a guided exploration to what moves you.

If your goal is to inspire others as well, then super! And let's be clear, we all have the ability to empower and motivate others to leave a positive footprint on the world. It simply starts with you!

You see, this book is really about life imitating art and showcasing the renewed sense that the learning experience is more holistic than ever before. There are characteristics, behaviours, and personalities that need to show up with every engagement you have with another human being. I'm going to substitute a human being with "audience." Your audience, no matter if it's one or 100,000, requires a new level of engagement from you. And that's going to require a shift in our thinking as individuals, professional facilitators, speakers, teachers, trainers, coaches, mentors, parents, lovers, husbands, wives, and any other persona that defines you in relation with another person.

You see, we're all looking to learn something from one another, so hopefully what we discuss in this book will set you up with the right habits and mindset to fulfil that need.

If you're wondering how I did in that class—yeah, I failed!

I wasn't ready to handle that level of psychological kung fu on humanity back then. But it was the agitation of that moment that stirred up my desire for exploration and set me on this path of discovery. *Even in failure comes success.*

WHAT I ENCOURAGE
YOU TO DO

Being in relationship with each other is no longer about just showing up. It has evolved into what people want and need from each other; which is a learning experience. With that in mind, one of my goals besides reminding you of your humanity, is taking you through a journey that focuses on psychological factors to increase the opportunity to learn from the most significant person in the room; yourself!

I'm going to refer to researchers, authors, musicians, poets, and all types of subject matter experts throughout this learning experience. Please understand, the lessons and life stories of individuals mentioned are not just by coincidence or because they sound compelling. Instead, they will help you know that there is a relationship between our experiences and our learning.

You will see numerous images throughout this book. What's important is that when you come to a piece of art, reflect on it before moving to the chapter and give yourself a moment to find out what that piece of art says to you. Then read the chapter. I would also recommend rereading the introduction after you have finished the book. I'd be curious to know if you come up with another understanding of what you learned about the book, the topic, the author, and most importantly, you!

Lastly, share your experience with me and others. Remember, we are all taking part in this relationship learning humanity journey together, and your thoughts matter.

All right, let's go!

1

Get to Know Your True Self

Bruce Lee
Credit image: unknown

"If you follow the classical pattern, you are understanding the routine, the tradition, the shadow -- you are not understanding yourself."
— **Bruce Lee, Tao of Jeet Kune Do**

Get to Know Your True Self

"Our connections to other human beings are not on the surface, but enveloped in the deepest parts of our pain, suffering, joy, faith, and spirit."

Sure, you may know of Bruce Lee, the martial artist and movie star. But do you know Bruce Lee, the philosopher, comedian and master of personal development?

Bruce was more than just an action star to me, but he was one of my earliest roles models. Although his physical prowess inspired bodybuilders and martial artists alike, the way in which he constantly pushed his mind to new levels inspired me from a young age to do the same.

As far as heroes go, Bruce Lee truly set an example of what it means to be YOUR best self.

Despite Bruce's drive and dedication to bettering himself, many took it to mean arrogant and unteachable. He didn't want to just limit himself to old systems and beliefs without challenging traditional thinking. Bruce wanted to expand his mind, so he sought guidance from some of the best teachers, philosophers and spiritual gurus, both living and dead.

Bruce was all about making the most of your life, seeking truth and knowledge, and applying what you learn to make a difference in the lives of others. If you've seen Bruce in movies or watched him being interviewed, you know precisely what his mantra was: Your blind spots can be your biggest weakness.

According to Bruce,

"After all, all knowledge simply means self-knowledge."

Who am I?

Ask yourself: *"Who am I?"*

Why should you do this, you might ask? Because through self-awareness, you will understand how to approach others and what you can give to them.

Aristotle stated,
> *"Knowing yourself is the beginning of all wisdom"* (Aristotle, 384-322 BC).

I've come to realize that while others feed off of your energy and enthusiasm, they can also sense your lack of authenticity.

If you don't believe in what you're saying, how and why should anyone else? If you're not willing to practice what you preach, eventually there will be a tug of war within your natural self and the self you choose to project to others. That's a lot of work trying to balance those two personas. We have to combine them, and that requires time for reflection and examination of the following:

What do I stand for? I stand for being true to myself and therefore, authentic with my audience, so there is little to no confusion regarding my convictions.

What are my habits? My habits are both predictable and subtle, slowly creeping into my life when I most need them.

Sometimes they can be intentionally ignored, but believe me when I tell you that my audience can quickly pick up on my tendencies. Consider your habits your "*poker play*" which I'll get into a bit later.

What are my tendencies? Like my habits, my inclinations are triggered by a feeling, a reaction, a need for survival. I like to believe that I am in control of my tendencies, but the truth is that they are in the driver's seat. If I'm honest, I'm terrified of my audience because they can be unrelenting and competitive.

What are my beliefs? I have to channel the best version of myself each time I'm in front of an audience. No two situations, circumstances, or spectators are the same in any sequence of life. What happens once is designed to happen in its unique way. No two people will receive the information the same way, so why would I deliver it the same way each time?

When you focus on your most faithful beliefs, those that are in your core, those that are most vulnerable to the outside, you create a heightened sense of worth. The value you place in that belief sets the tone to how far your message will carry.

How do I feel at this moment? I feel as vulnerable as I should. The more vulnerable I feel, the more I seem to deliver my true self and more importantly, the more my audience tends to hear, retain, and act on their behalf. I'm here to change how people feel about themselves so that they feel empowered to do more, be more, learn more, experience more, and change more.

These are sample questions that getting to know yourself allows you to explore. As you can tell, the truth that lies within these types of questions exposes you, and it will feel a bit uncomfortable as you explore the answers.

Alice Miller wrote, "*We can repair ourselves and gain our lost integrity by choosing to look more closely at the knowledge that is stored inside our bodies and bringing this knowledge closer to our awareness.*"

Personally, I interpret this to mean that our pure goodness is in our brokenness. Understanding this is a requirement for growth. What matters is the story that we're able to tell because of our personal experiences.

Our connections to other human beings are not on the surface but enveloped in the deepest parts of our pain, suffering, joy, faith, and spirit. When we unlock those imperfection areas, we recapture a higher sense of self, allowing our genuine authenticity to peak through. It is liberating and reassuring not just for self but to those that get to experience that level of courage with us. Yes, I used the word courage because only by conquering your fear, will you get to this level of transparency. Your audience will appreciate it more, and you'll find that your teaching will go much further with your audience.

What do I mean by an audience?

In the learning and development profession, where I've spent a good portion of my professional career, I have come to believe that the people I interact with are my audience. They're not white, black, Asian, Hispanic, short, dark, tall, fit, fat, or otherwise. They are human beings. Now, it can be an audience of 1 or 100,000. In every instance, this individual(s) has voluntarily or involuntarily chosen to give me their time and energy with the hope of gaining some personally identified benefit.

My audience can be a family member, a friend, a peer, a colleague, or a group of strangers. It doesn't matter where they come from or who they are, but I consider it my responsibility to treat them with the attention and care that someone who wants to learn deserves. That simply means being present, paying attention, and responding to their cues. When you see me reference the word "audience," it's important to understand that we each have a unique audience of individuals who require something from us. Treat them as you would want to be treated and empower them to be able to walk away from you feeling "okay."

Back to Reality

Your reality is simple; for better or worse, this is how "I" think, these are "my" biases, and these are "my" strengths and weaknesses. We are doing ourselves a favor when we're able to examine ourselves better. We're taking a load off our shoulders when we no longer have to pretend to be something that we aren't. We become more human, and people like to relate to human.

H – helping
U – unite
M – minds
A – and
N – needs

Being what we *are* and pretending to act like the person we are *not,* can be a struggle, especially trying to keep the two personas separate. It requires much effort, an intentional willingness, incredible patience, and a bit of constant apologizing. (Apologies need forgiveness and we'll tackle forgiveness a bit later in the journey). It's a struggle between light and dark, a seesaw of emotions that move one way or another.

You're in constant battle, and the central problem could be our lack of an inner compass. As Bill George, bestselling author of *True North,* would say, "We have a 360-degree vision but no true north." Our accurate compass is merely about rediscovering what makes us authentic, and that is what will guide you in your relationships, your search for humanity, and your ability to have real relationships.

In my case, it's empowering people to think for themselves and problem-solve issues through professional development, coaching, mentoring, and supporting their best-laid plan for themselves. What will rediscovering your true self do for you?

Why should this matter?

Think about your favourite movie, favourite book, favourite meal, or favourite anything. The one thing that you can point back to is humanity in the character, the soul in which the food was prepared, and the story that allowed you to connect in a new way. Those were kick-ass moments, and we love them! The golden thread that captured us from all walks of life are the elements of being human, and that's what drives engagement. The more human you become to your audience, the greater chance you have of creating a learning environment where everyone thrives. That's why I love keeping it real with my audience. It's part of my journey, and those real-world experiences of winning, losing, and suffering are all weaved into the fabric of what it is that I have to offer. These are our life stories, and expressing them in our fabulous and unique ways frees the soul and gives your spirit a place to soar.

Quick story

When Bruce was young, he pushed his sister Phoebe into a swimming pool as a joke, and she responded by holding his head underwater until he promised never to do it again. From then on, he never went into a swimming pool again. The notion of Mr. Lee not wanting to go back into the pool may seem minuscule to most, but on a deeper level, Bruce knew himself well enough not to train or do any scenes near water. He was self-aware of his fears, biases, limitations, etc., and that level of honesty and transparency with himself made him that much more effective. He conquered his fears by being more aware of them. It may seem difficult to grasp at first, but as we continue on this journey, you will discover this very meaningful message that will change the trajectory of your life.

The power in this story lies behind Bruce's willingness to be self-aware of his flaws. That's what we remember, and that's why his legacy continues to be so strong today. I don't know about you, but I want my impact on this world to be felt long after I'm gone so that my story can continue in someone else's life. When you teach, train, mentor, coach, and guide, there should be a sense of duality. Yes, I want to stay in the present, practise mindfulness, and prepare my audience for an immediate "can-do" ability. Still, I also want them to learn the most important lesson that will shape their lives forever. True-self!

There's so much to learn about yourself and others when your actions speak louder than your words alone. In the next chapter, we will explore what it means to express yourself in a genuine way that shows why you care about what you do. As I mentioned, my talent is Learning and Development, but yours may be cooking, running a gym, building maintenance, leading a youth program, or managing the family structure at home. What you choose to do is not the focus. How you do it is!

2

Actions Show What You Care About

Eleanor Roosevelt
Credit image: unknown

"We are afraid to care too much, for fear that the other person does not care at all."

~ Eleanor Roosevelt

Actions Show What You Care About

"I had to re-program what caring for something else and someone else looked like in practice."

When Eleanor Roosevelt turned fifteen, her grandmother sent her to a boarding school close to London. Eleanor was scared at first and very reclusive, but the headmistress, Mademoiselle Marie Souvestre, took a particular interest in her and subsequently had a significant influence over the intellectual development of Roosevelt. Souvestre demonstrated an independence of mind, scholarly accomplishment, and during those times, a commitment to human justice. Her actions were considered highly abnormal and not necessarily the "place" for a woman.

Roosevelt would later write, "Observing the model of Souvestre, I think I came to feel that the underdog was always the one to be championed."

Seeing her headmistress champion human justice causes, especially for woman, gave her the courage and confidence to develop her own voice. By the time she graduated, Eleanor had not only become more confident, but she learned more about herself and her purpose in life. She became more self-aware.

When Eleanor's formal education ended at age 18, she would begin her social reform work soon. She served as a volunteer teacher for impoverished immigrant children at Manhattan's Rivington Street Settlement House. Afterwards, Eleanor joined the National Consumers' League, whose mission was to end unsafe working conditions and labour practices in factories and other businesses. Her actions demonstrated to others what she cared about and those actions inspired others.

A Need for Self-preservation

I grew up in the Crown Heights area of Brooklyn, NY. Although life at a young age was complicated, the simplicity of my daily outlook was not. I needed to avoid the neighbourhood gangsters, bullies, and addicts. I also cared about things like Wrestle Mania, GI Joe, Jamaican beef patties, Chico sticks, Bon Ton chips, Welches grape soda, and putting a high score on Mike Tyson's Punch-Out at one of the bodegas on Kingston Ave (shout out to Manny and Gloria!)

Laugh now, but for those that can relate, Bon Ton chips were on point. I had older brothers, friends, extended family, enemies of all kinds, but what mattered to me was managing the chaos in my dysfunctional home life. Trying to stay a few steps ahead of dangers lurking on the block, and finding ways to keep the basic necessities within arm's reach. As I mentioned, complicated but simple!

To stay a few steps ahead, I mastered the art of influence. I didn't have to be the loud talker, but a smooth operator. I could work a room just by observing the players present, making a quick assessment, and being prepared to implement a plan to guarantee my need for a simple outcome.

I later realized that I had what others called "a presence."

Some of the rules of managing dysfunction and chaos where I grew up weren't always legitimate, but, in my mind, they were necessary. Unlike Eleanor Roosevelt, I was self-serving in every way. I cared only about *"meeeeeee,"* and clearly expressed this to everyone I came in contact with.

When it came to working with others in a professional capacity, this selfish attitude followed me. Heck, it even followed me throughout my personal relationships. I came to realize far too often that my mentality was counterproductive and destructive. I couldn't sustain the premise that caring about me was the only way I could express myself.

I had to re-program what caring for something else and someone else looked like in practice.

Sure, you can read books, watch compelling stories, go to church even, but none of those things will stick with you unless you start to experience them for yourself. In other words, I had to choose a new attitude! That required taking all the bullshit I accepted, getting my hands dirty, and pulling out the things that mattered from the pile of crap I was handed. You see, even the shit tells a story. That's why doctors say you should always take a look at your stool once you've finished doing #2. Sorry, back to the story.

Fast Forward

Here's a bit of scientific reference to bore you a bit more. Researchers Kahn (1990), and Truss et al. (2006) define engagement as 'passion for work,' a psychological state which encompasses the three dimensions of engagement. I won't get into the three dimensions of engagement. I will leave that up to you. Another researcher,

Saks (2006), suggests that commitment differs from engagement in that it refers to a person's attitude and attachment toward their agenda. In other words, there is a direct correlation between an individual's engagement or attentiveness to their mission and the perceived outcome. This relationship between labour and love creates what I believe to be a "flow," or as Csikszentmihalyi might say, "Holistic sensation that people feel when they act with total involvement" (Csikszentmihalyi 1975:36). So why am I telling you this?

Think about the work that you love to do. No, not the work that you're paid to do (although if you're lucky, maybe it's the same). Nevertheless, when you genuinely love and have a passion for what you do, it no longer becomes a chore. It no longer matters who is watching. It no longer reads like a billboard sign. *It becomes you!*

You are a walking, talking, acting, feeling billboard. I always hated the question when I would network and meet new people, "So, what do you for work?" I would hear people respond with this barrage of words filled with tasks and activities that far exceeded what was necessary. Meanwhile, between my gentle head nods and seemingly interested look, my attention would almost always be focused on the snack tray that's been going around the room. . Them sliders tho!

If I go back to Csikszentmihalyi for a second, individuals in a "flow" experience need no external rewards or goals to motivate them. The idea is that the activity itself presents constant challenges that create engagement that changes lives. Your ability to show how and why you care about what you do is the special sauce that makes the meal authentic and desirable. On the flip side, when we're disconnected in our daily relationships, it becomes evident that we're merely going through the motions. Your audience will sense that quickly, and we lose a significant opportunity for learning to take place.

Ask yourself these three fundamental questions as you start to dissect where you are in your learning journey to understand where you are searching for humanity and discover the impact you choose to have in your relationships. (i) How meaningful is it for me to bring myself into this production; (ii) How safe is it to do so? (iii) How available am I to do so?

Meaning and Production

You might have noticed vital terms up to this point, such as meaning and production. Something to keep in mind is that I like to also refer to meaning as a purpose. As an individual whose goal is to impact the minds of people and challenge them to better their personal growth, I derive meaning or purpose from the very nature of that work. To see others improve their lives through learning is a positive, motivating force within my life. A person's perception of "meaning" in the workplace is connected to how engaged they are and their performance (Holbeche and Springett 2003).

Is teaching, training, coaching, or mentoring, a labour of love or just labour? To sacrifice your ego, you have to be able to separate yourself from your personal goals for the well-being of others, especially those looking for guidance. Eleanor Roosevelt provides a perfect example. If most of your time is spent talking about your experiences, talking about your goals, talking about your mission, then you and your audience will quickly lose sight of the desired destination. Replace "I" and "my" with "we." In other words, bring those individuals listening to you along with you. Include them in your passion and make it infectious for everyone. This is the best type of infection to have, especially when built from a real place.

Be excited, engaging, elaborative, and unapologetically engulfed. There's only one way to bring to life the message that you want your audience to learn. The more they see how you are living the message, flexing the muscles of the message, and hosting the message within yourself, then the more they will take from it. We have an inherent desire to feel connected to what we're learning, or it won't take. Maslow's Hierarchy of Needs diagram proves relevant here. At the base of the pyramid is the need for warmth, food, shelter, and sleep. Once those needs are met, we progress towards this need for safety and security. As people progress up the pyramid, needs become increasingly psychological and social, which is where this topic makes its most significant impact.

The ability to effortless demonstrate to others why you care so much about what you do really lands on your level of self-awareness. I've heard folks say that you have to get comfortable with the uncomfortable to transform your inner self into your outer self. Once that transformation happens, it's challenging to dispute your intentions because your transparency level rises to new levels.

I can only express my real self if I know myself.

Keep in mind this golden thread that will be interwoven throughout all the perspectives that you learn about while immersing yourself in the book. Think about Chapter One and use this as the next essential element necessary to create a system that changes the way you move in your relationships. I can only speak for the excellent care that I have in what I do because I know how it made a difference in the many lives I've been able to learn with and from. But ask yourself, what is that "I" care about? Is it the work that I do, the nature of how I do it, or the outcomes as a result of what I do?

Quick story

Eleanor was the very first First Lady to ever hold a press conference. She held it with an all-women press corps, which gave a great deal of prestige to the female White House correspondents. They were able to cover issues concerning national and international affairs as presented by the First Lady. This press conference was a brilliant act of solidarity with the Women's Rights Movement. Still, it also gave Eleanor an independent avenue to report on matters that were near to her heart without any filtering. Her excitement around what she was and what she'd become gave her the courage to change the status quo, and it allowed others to feed off of that energy. She became her message so that those in attendance could find their inner strengths and exhibit their own bravery.

When you exhibit that level of care, it becomes evident to observers, near and far, as to what you're about. They no longer must ask because anything short of just watching and listening answers all those questions. I had to make that evolution, which is the only reason I'm here today, sharing these stories and experiences.

I was willing to stunt my intellectual growth and maturity by focusing on the words I used and not the actions behind those words. That was not the type of impact I wanted to be remembered. Instead, I found clarity of what mattered when fighting for something. And what mattered in those moments are the folks that needed an encouraging word, a kind act, a selfless deed, a loud voice, some food for thought, and a genuine person with an infectious spirit.

In those moments, *I found my Eleanor Roosevelt.*

In the next chapter, we take an inward look at what can determine legacy impact status in relationships. I find that the better I can navigate through the bullshit that lurks from within, the better I can help others chart a cleaner path. The sacrifice that is made is more of personal pride and prejudice.

3

Start from Within and Work Your Way Out

Ruth Bader Ginsberg
Credit image: unknown

"Fight for the things that you care about but do it in a way that will lead others to join you."

~ **Ruth Bader Ginsburg** (Rest in Power!)

Start from Within and Work Your Way Out

"You're here to help others be better, not so that you can look better."

One of the greatest inspirations I have come to know is Ruth Bader Ginsburg, aka "Notorious RBG". She served as a shining example of strength, persistence, equality, and fairness. So where did her inspiration come from?

Celia Bader, née Amster, Ruth's mother, died the day before Ginsburg's high school graduation. But in their short time together, Celia managed to instill in her daughter that education was not something to be taken for granted. Celia herself, whom Ginsburg regularly called the most intelligent person she'd ever known, went to work at age 15 to help put her brother through college.

At the 1993 White House press conference announcing her nomination to the Supreme Court, Ginsburg wrapped up her remarks with an emotional tribute to the woman whose life was cut short before reaching her full potential. "I have a last thank you," she told the crowd assembled.

> *"It's from my mother. My mother was the bravest, strongest person I have ever known, who was taken from me much too soon. I pray that I may be all that she would have been had she lived in an age when women could aspire and achieve, and daughters are cherished as much as sons."*

RBG's mother may not have had the academic pedigree, wealth, and riches to pass down to her daughter, but she did the most with what she did have. She did more and became more so that others could be better. It's this level of commitment to serving a greater purpose is what separates you having a fleeting moment impact on someone life versus one that leaves a legacy impression.

Read the Room

Researchers refer to our ability to connect with others and recognize social and psychological needs in each other as conversational intelligence. Conversational Intelligence® (C-IQ) translates this awareness into conversations that meet these needs. It acknowledges people's social and psychological needs and celebrates when conditions are met.

When I am delivering a presentation, workshop, or coaching session, I make it a point to scan the audience every three minutes to see if anyone is showing signs of checking out. I know individuals that consider it a personal offense when someone loses interest in what they have to say. We tend to think that anybody who does this is uncooperative or unreasonable, which can lead to counterproductive behaviors on our part. We begin to pound our point home or simply ignore them and focus on the other participants in the room. All counterproductive!

We are present to help others be better, not so that we can look better. Somehow, we have gotten this idea that people are actually there to see us and that it's all about "me." We fall into this "ego" trap that every word, movement, mannerism, and expression that we make becomes the trigger that changes their lives forever.

We rehearse, go over our lines, jokes, taglines, and all of that to get the perfect reaction from our audience. The vanity of it all is that we believe it just has to be perfect. We become so absorbed on the *"I"* component that we quickly lose sight of what our audience wants. Why?

We hate to stray from our plan. It requires too much effort to speak with our audience as opposed to talk at them. We learn to perfect our insecurities, imperfections, and quirks over the many experiences of what seems to be acceptable based on what we perceive to be our worth. We think our "one size fits all" speech in a box should do the job. Our words of wisdom are the golden ticket. Besides, if everyone can't learn at least one thing from me, there must be something wrong with them. Wow!

The vicious cycle we just created of declining engagement and expressing annoyance will continue until the tension is relieved. The truth is that all people have innate needs for meaning, purpose, and connection that they want and expect to fulfill. It's part of the relationship-building process.

By definition, relationships are bidirectional, with each person giving and receiving.

Sure, this seems obvious on the surface, but it becomes more difficult in practice. As individuals, we are each born with a plan. We may not discover our purpose for many years after our birth, but as we grow, learn, and develop from experiences, we figure out how to settle into our convictions. We then meet someone else who has their own set of beliefs, and so begins the gentle game of tug-of-war to build a connection.

Adjust before it is too late

Adjust your style so that others feel motivated. It can be difficult to adjust when you're fixed in your thinking. Being agile and flexible is vital to being useful in any capacity. But it's also a solid foundation for being human.

We're learning to be adaptable to our audiences' needs, especially if you want them to keep coming back. Don't sell yourself short thinking that you're in that room by yourself and for yourself. You've got a conglomerate of eager minds looking to share in a learning experience with you. So why not make it worth everyone's time?

Yes, it takes courage! It is nothing that impossible that you can't overcome. Take comfort in your level of discomfort because we all grow when that happens.

Quick story

Ginsburg reflected on landmark women's rights cases that she worked on when she first became a justice in the 1970s. "The object was to get at a stereotype that held women back from doing whatever their talent would allow them to do," she said. "The notion was that there were separate spheres for the sexes. Men were the doers in the world, and women were the stay-at-home types." She later added that now is a better time than any women to go after what they want. "Young women today have a great advantage, and it is that there are no more closed doors," Ginsburg said. "That was basically what the '70s were all about. Opening doors that had been closed to women."

The Supreme Court Justice's message to young girls was simple yet powerful: "Fight for the things that you care about, but do it in a way that will lead others to join you." Ruth Bader Ginsburg's willingness to care for the well-being of others is not merely human, but a staple in the occupation that I love.

The ability to inspire starts from within and works its way out. This is what I have to exhibit each time I interact with another person. It's no longer a choice but a way of life and therefore becomes entrenched in how I treat others with my actions and words, and equally important, how I treat myself.

In the next chapter, we grapple with the power of words. The power of words comes into play during the times when we define our reality. The words we use in our minds repeatedly to describe ourselves and our identity are some of the most potent forces in our lives.

4

Understand the Power of Words

"Raise your words, not your voice. It is rain that grows flowers, not thunder." ~ Rumi

Understand the Power of Words

"Her name was Olivia Hernandez, and she was the embodiment of rock star meets hip hop meets sugar and spice and everything nice."

Rumi Writings
Credit image: unknown

More than seven centuries after his death, Jalal al Din Mohammad Rumi's poetry still fascinates and inspires his readers. The 13th-century Sufi theologian and poet is one of America's best-selling poets, with his work being read at weddings, performed by artists and musicians in cramped Brooklyn basements, and endlessly quoted on Instagram.

But few people know much about the man behind these timeless lines of poetry. In Brad Gooch's book, "Rumi's Secret: The Life of the Sufi Poet of Love," Gooch seeks to give modern readers a glimpse into Rumi's life by studying the poet's travels and his spiritual formation. Gooch told "The Huffington Post" that, like many others, he was fascinated by the beautiful and sensual imagery in Rumi's poetry.

It is in Rumi's words that moves so many of us that follow his work like a thunderous wave tossing a ship in whatever direction it pleases.

What words do

It is safe to assume that we've all heard or even used the phrase, "talk is cheap," right? I like to say that talk is cheap, but the consequences can be expensive. This is especially true if you're not prepared to back up those words with action or even worse, don't take into consideration the impact those words will have on others' lives.

I recall the first time I told another person, "I love you." Her name was Olivia Hernandez, and she was the embodiment of rock star meets hip hop meets sugar and spice and everything nice. She had long brown hair, a button nose, and full lips. Damn, I can see her so clearly now, albeit this was over twenty-five years ago.

Truthfully, I don't know if I actually loved Olivia because I was too young to have a real understanding of what love meant. I didn't feel love growing up with my parents. I didn't hear those words as a child. I only knew what I saw on TV and what I heard on the radio.

What I did know was that Olivia came from a broken home and that she liked the attention. Olivia was a Scorpio and had plenty of spice to go with her temper. She was angry a lot, finding drama as quickly as drama found her. She was only thirteen, and yet she knew so much about how the world worked. Olivia set her sights on me, and for all intents and purposes, she liked me. The more time I spent with her, the more I learned to use persuasive words to keep her near.

I would make promises to go places with her, buy her things, protect her honour, and most importantly, love her. Unfortunately, I couldn't follow through on any of these things because I was merely a street kid trying to manage dysfunction and chaos, jumping from one hustle to another. Remember Chapter One?

My talk was cheap, but Olivia bought into my words as if I were the Pied Piper. Once she realized and accepted the fact that I could not deliver, she moved on. She went to another public school in Brooklyn, and I never ran into her again. I was such an ass!

Words empower, words encourage, but more importantly, words should provoke thought. I didn't realize how critical words were until I started to interact with different cultures from around the world. Your words mean different things to everybody, making it all the more important to choose purposeful, action-oriented words that provoke emotion to elicit a response.

The fact is, once we read or examine a linguistic structure, our attention goes in two directions at once. We are trying to make sense of the words we are reading, while simultaneously trying to recall the conventional meanings of the terms outside the word being read. Northrop Frye describes this dynamic as two structures: the structure of what is being told and the structure of the words describing it. The point is that words are complicated, lethal, habit-forming, and in some forms, a contradiction to action.

We constantly struggle with deciphering their meaning and purpose, especially if not used with good intention.

When I first started in my career, I would often mimic others in the business who I thought were masterful at using their words. Not just their words but their inflexion, tone, and cadence. I would get mesmerized by speakers and study them as if I were preparing for a final exam. There is an obsessive side of my personality that enables me to fixate and truly study a person. It is a side that I have fully embraced, especially in my career.

Nonetheless, I knew how important it was for them to capture these massive audiences with their words. The speed with which they spoke was engaging, and I never walked away from them confused about what they were trying to convey. Well, the same goes for me now. People always tell me how they love the way that I talk, and they could listen to me all day. I used to be flattered by that, but then I understood it was more than just me; it was my words and how they made them feel.

Understand this: your audience wants to feel something when they engage with you. Our job is to teach, coach, empower and motivate, so that action is generated as a result. All of these words I mention are action words, and therefore we must understand their power. The same can be said about the improper use of words and what it can do to an audience.

Words deflate, debilitate, and delay learning

I'm sure many of us have sat in a conference, classroom, seminar, or at the dinner table, and just felt utterly removed from the conversation. The experience itself may have even created some negative habits and mindsets. Understanding words requires having a sensitivity regarding diversity and inclusion. If you don't know what I mean by that, then let me elaborate.

Diversity is not just about our differences in appearance, sex, race, origin, or ethnicity. It's also about the different experiences we all bring to the table. Those experiences shape our opinions, our behaviours, and our mannerisms. We form our identity from our diversity. We tend to believe what we do is based on our diversity, and if we aren't sensitive to that, then our words will exclude critical people you're trying to connect with. The inclusion part requires not just an understanding of our various experiences and backgrounds, but more importantly, how to make those differences part of our messaging. Now, that takes practice!

Words can derail your plan

I remember running a workshop on Emotional Intelligence, and I started to talk about the concept of self-awareness. Now, self-awareness is a critical component to self-actualization and fulfilment because it helps you connect with yourself on a higher level of acceptance. However, what I failed to realize was that the word "self-actualization" means something significant in certain faiths. It's sacred to some and should not be used lightly. I believe one person in the room spoke up and brought up religion and faith as I started to talk about the concept. My intent wasn't to have a religious discussion, but that terminology invoked a spiritual trigger in this particular person, and it could not be overlooked.

Now the focus had suddenly shifted from emotional intelligence to a discussion between attendees on faith and religion. If you ever want to get into a spirited debate, start dancing around the topic of faith and religion. It can be just as passionate as a discussion on politics. My failure to carefully choose my words, paired with the lack of context or intent I had meant them in, created palpable tension in the room. That, in turn, took the focus away from the workshop on this essential critical skill. Lesson learned!

Quick story

The map of Rumi's life stretched over 2500 miles as his family's migration lasted nearly two decades. Rumi's family travelled from Vakhsh to Samarkand in Uzbekistan, Iran, Syria, Saudi Arabia, and finally to Turkey, where Rumi spent the last 50 years of his life. The experience of moving exposed Rumi to many different languages and religious practices. "He was truly migrant in this sense of passing through all these places. You see it in the impermanence of things embraced in Rumi's poetry," Gooch said.

Those experiences were a huge advantage for Rumi, as they allowed him to express himself with universally accepted words in today's world. However, I argue that it was more than just his words, but also his desire to use those words as a means of bringing people together, empowering them to think, and enabling them to take action as a result. There is a willingness that goes along with the practice of understanding the power of words.

In the next chapter, we take a subtle shift from using our words to actively listening so that others feel involved. A willingness to involve others requires patience, but that gets your audience closer to embracing your ideas. An engaged and involved audience will simply be more willing to be influenced by you.

5

Allow Your Audience to Participate

Lincoln Theatre Washington DC
Credit image: Bear and Bailey Productions

"Neither you nor your audience should feel captive. It shouldn't be a chore to listen, but a desire to engage." - "Bear" Bailey

Allow Your Audience to Participate

"We're provided two ears and one mouth for more than just aesthetics.
"

In what I consider to be my roaring twenties, I did an awful job of pretending to be human (H.U.M.A.N.). Ironically, I was so bad at it, that I was considered good to the outside world. I was what one would call a functional addict. Yes, I was solid at my work, and I appeared to have it all together. But what folks didn't realize about me was that I was self-serving. Let me explain my addiction.

My personnel would applaud my behaviour because of the level of intensity and focus I could display, regardless of the situation. My activity and behaviour became the primary focus of my life, to the point where I simply excluded other activities. It didn't matter if my conduct had the potential to harm another individual physically, mentally, or socially. If you were around me during my twenties, I would get a thrill from playing the shell game. It became an obsession filled with compulsive behaviour.

My addiction was self! I was obsessed with myself, and whether you chose to play along or watch from the sidelines, it was always about what I could get out of the situation.

That type of addiction does not allow your audience to take part in a mutually beneficial manner. It is only about you! This is painful just sharing this level of transparency, but it is necessary for bringing back the humanity I needed for me to flourish in my relationships.

Listening should not be a chore

We're provided with two ears and one mouth for more than just aesthetics. I've heard people say it's because we need to listen twice as much as we talk, but how else can I be heard?

Remember, I'm an expert in this scenario. I know what's best, and I'm going to prove it by talking the most. Plus, I'm from Brooklyn—fuhgeddaboudit!

All joking aside, this is a dangerous game that we see played far too often. We see it in our politics, we see it in churches, we see it in our school administrators, and we see it at home.

As a parent, I've reinforced the notion that "*Dad is always right.*" It doesn't matter if you have an opinion or not. Just know that at the beginning, middle, and end of the day, say it with me now, "*Dad is always right.*"

The ego and arrogance to believe that to be true is indeed a mistake. The heart and soul of the matter rely on the inability to recognize when the truth is being spoken. There is a tendency to associate talking the most, talking the loudest, and interrupting while someone else is talking, as showing control. I needed to feel like I was in control, and what better way to do that than to maintain control of the message?

The problem occurs when your audience begins to tune out your message. The individual comes to realize that nothing she says will be heard, and if she can't be heard, why should she participate? It's even more painful as a spectator watching someone go down this path, only to realize that it's too late. You can't get out, you've gotten lost, and the audience that could have been your lifeline has gone away. I've participated in all areas of the scenario mentioned above, and it's always painful.

In my relationships, nothing is worse than sitting and trying to listen without engagement. You want to participate, turn it into a discussion, and maybe make a good point here and there, but nothing! Neither you nor your audience should feel captive. It shouldn't be a chore to listen, but a desire to engage.

It matters how your audience receives what you're selling so that they can personalize it and make it work for them. The more your audience participates, the less memorization required. This will naturally result in higher engagement levels, including interpretation, analysis, and synthesis (Smith, 1977). If that's not the approach, your message will be quickly forgotten as soon as the next distraction comes along.

You can improve your audience's working memory level if you make an intentional effort to get those in attendance to participate in the learning. In other words, pull them, rather than push them along.

Participation is a way to bring your intended audience actively into the learning process, as well as assist in "enhancing our teaching and bringing life to the lesson" (Cohen, 1991, p. 699). People are generally more motivated, learn better, become better critical thinkers, and have self-reported character gains—all of this just from allowing your audience to participate in the discussions.

Pull

This idea of "pulling" focuses on getting your audience to contribute to the focal point of the message, conversation, and debate. You bring him along the journey to be always engaged and more importantly, given the opportunity to participate. Whenever I would look to design, develop, or curate content, I always looked for insight from those that would be impacted by my work. In other words, their opinions mattered! They are the ones that would be using the "product." They are the ones that would have to "*buy-in*" to what was being presented. How else would you know if what you're building is working? You can't!

My experiences show me that participation can be seen as an active engagement process, sorted into categories. University of Sydney professors Diane Dancer and Patty Kamvounias eloquently named them for us: preparation, contribution to a discussion, group skills, communication skills, and attendance. I've found that all of these areas, as mentioned earlier, are impacted significantly when I make a concerted effort to address them.

Part of what will make you successful in communicating is measuring the impact on learners as they engage with your content. Learners will not engage if they do not recognize it. Times are changing, especially when learning can happen more abundantly than at any other time in our history. Learning occurs at the touch of a button or the stroke of a key. Knowledge and content are pulled from social media, media outlets, TV programs, blogs, etc.

You have no real control over where people get their information from, so your chances of losing them increases. Quite frankly, there is a lot of noise out there. There are ten ways to do everything, and everyone thinks they have something new or profound to add to the mix. Heck, I wrote this book as a testament to that!

Nonetheless, as you develop content, don't underestimate the authoring ability of your audience. Many of them may come to the table, believing that they already know more than you. Why? They have read it somewhere before. Here is my solution. Take time to understand your audience and "pull" from them what they believe they know. Create your conversations around what your audience knows to allow themselves to learn something new. Listen twice as much as you talk!

Push

The opposite of "pulling" is "pushing," which most of us in unequally yoked relationships tend to do. You don't need to be in my chosen occupation to do this, because most of us like telling others what to do. We believe we are the subject matter experts; we have our doctorates, accolades, research, and other commercial items that make us feel important. We say we know better and we push our message on our audience. In the classroom, I call it "talking at you."

As I'm talking *at* you, guess what, I'm also alienating you, shutting down the possibility of learning from you, ignoring your diversity, and excluding your contribution.

Everything that I mentioned not to do in earlier chapters. Remember, these are the building blocks to use as you create the type of human aka "learner" you want to be in life, and in your chosen calling.

Quick story

Musicians are probably the best example to illustrate this topic. Their rifts inspire, their words excite, and their hooks enlighten. The good ones find a way to get us to participate regardless of the genre. Think about the number of songs you know how to sing along to. That's no accident or a coincidence. As a matter of opinion, I would think it's the musician's goal. Should it be ours?

We bring our audience along the journey, and they will remember what we taught them long after we've gone our separate ways.

In the next chapter, we take a willingness to listen a bit further by empowering what others say to you to help them help themselves. It's my position that every person should be the architect of his or her own fortune. In your relationships, you will quickly find that everyone may not have the building material needed, but you can play a critical part in helping them use the tools they do have.

6

Help Them to Teach Themselves

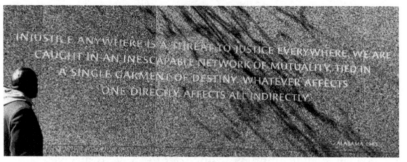

Martin Luther King, Jr. Memorial Washington DC
Image credit: Bear and Bailey Productions

*"The function of education is to teach one
to think intensively and to think critically.
Intelligence plus character - that is the goal
of true education."* ~ Martin Luther King, Jr.

Help Them to Teach Themselves

"People with high assurance in their capabilities approach difficult tasks as challenges to be mastered rather than as threats to be avoided."

Martin Luther King, Jr. was, among many things, a social activist and Baptist minister who played a vital role in the American Civil Rights Movement from the mid-1950s until his assassination in 1968. King sought equality and human rights for African Americans, the economically disadvantaged, and all victims of injustice through peaceful protest.

King argued that education has both a practical and a moral function.

I believe King used all that precious knowledge to teach others how to become self-sufficient, how to think for themselves, how to maneuver in a system designed to alienate them, how to exhibit pride over prejudice, and most importantly, how to survive.

Each one teaches one

Have you ever watched water flow downstream? I mean really watched and wondered about its movement, the pattern, the places it touched, what is left behind, where it was going, and what the end goal would be once it got to its destination?

As I go through this mental exercise, what is revealed to me, is that the 'end' goal as we define it is really just the start. Nothing truly has an end but merely another beginning where all things flourish again. Each time that water crashes along the side of an embankment, each time it washes onto a rock, it pulls something in with it and then spits it back out, it is helping something else get what it needs. The grasses, wildflowers, and land animals are being nourished.

Toxins and other hazardous material that we callously disregard is being taken away so that life within the water gets adequately nourished. Rocks and barriers are slowly being transformed, leaving and taking away nutrients and minerals to be distributed somewhere else. I know this may sound like a lot of Zen-type thinking, but everything that we encounter is designed to teach us something, and that lesson should not just be hoarded by one, but rather, it should be channelled into others so that we all may benefit from those encounters. Now that the Lao Tzu portion of the program has been covered let's move into some efficacy findings (i.e. the boring part of the program).

Self-efficacy

Perceived self-efficacy is defined as a person's belief about their capabilities to produce a certain level of performance, in so much as they can then exercise this performance over events in their lives. Now that is a mouthful, so I'm going to try to simplify the message. Self-efficacy determines how people *feel, think, behave* and *motivate* themselves. A strong sense of efficacy enhances human accomplishment and personal well-being in many ways.

People with high assurance in their capabilities approach difficult tasks as challenges to be mastered rather than as threats to be avoided.

Our company recently conducted a study on learner improvement and whether participants felt what they had experienced in a formal learning environment could be used to improve their lives. Among the most commonly reported areas of feedback was that 88% of respondents agreed that they acquired knowledge about a new subject, 85% saw applications for their work, and 78% agreed the learning experience also improved abilities to make scientifically informed decisions at work.

Our findings suggested that we were taking the right approach in helping our learners teach themselves—almost a train-the-trainer of sorts approach.

So, as you navigate your own personal journey, I suggest you do the following things:

- **Continue to ask**: *Can your learner teach someone else what you taught them?* Can they spread your message further and wider than the confines of the classroom, the office, the living room, the kitchen, the gym, or the virtual space where learning happens? Are you building your interactions with individuals in a way where you become obsolete? The term obsolete is not necessarily a bad thing, especially if you give someone the skills they need to make a difference in their personal and professional lives.
- **Think more deeply about it**: why wouldn't you want empowered individuals capable of using what you are teaching them not just for their lives, but also for the people influenced by them? How more powerful is the message when it can be carried effortlessly downstream without losing its impact,

purpose, and position? My plan is simple: help you to think for yourself. What's the old proverb, "*Give a man a fish, and you feed him for a day. Teach a man to fish, and you feed him for a lifetime.*" Wow, how powerful is that if you go into your day with that mindset?

Thinking and being in this mental space is a skill that takes practice. Sure, some of us are gifted with that ability, but for most of us, it takes work. Thinking has almost become a lost art because so many decisions are made for us these days. We no longer think about what we're going to eat because there's an app for that. We don't have to think about what to wear because there's an app for that. We don't necessarily have to leave the house anymore where a lot of thinking needs to happen. There's an app for that!

Unfortunately, when faced with a dire need to think and decide, many of us are left paralyzed or hesitant by the thought because we're simply out of practice.

You've heard the term muscle atrophy, right? If you're not able to use or choose not to use a particular muscle(s) in your body, then it will get weaker, smaller, and less functional. Now those muscles don't disappear; they simply become dormant. I like to consider the brain one of our biggest, strongest, fastest, and most bionic muscles. When used often, challenged consistently, and nourished with the right stimuli, its functionality can be quite astounding. Just thinking about what it has meant for me brings joy to my heart. When you help others better use their brain muscles, you're building self-assurance, security, safety, survival, and shelter.

It can be demoralizing, so it should become a natural responsibility to help people re-engage their minds, so they feel empowered again. You're providing a lesson on reconnecting with humanity. That serves as a catalyst for a higher purpose. Besides, it's also a relief for you!

Don't carry the load, share in it

I mentioned that it's a relief for you and the truth is, you don't have to carry the load by yourself. Instead, you can share it! Learning has to take place organically, in a situation where both parties' antennas are receptive to cues and messaging that triggers thought. Once you start carrying the pressure of having an audience unable to feed themselves and always needing more because you failed to teach them how to think critically on their own—that's more than you should handle!

It's part of the changing dynamics of the craft. It's no longer acceptable for a learner to just show up because we are all looking for more than that. We're looking for an experience that connects us back to our humanity. They're looking to gain mastery with every interaction they have with us.

The attention spans continue to shrink, the requirements are just as high, and the time allocated for formal learning is shortened. Everything is faster, more compact, and with the same implications as before, if not more drastic. We've got a captive audience, and we have to make the most out of it. That's why we have to design ourselves, our programs, our workshops, and our interactions based on the learner's needs. How do you want to learn? How do you want to engage? If you desire to connect with what's in front of you or around you more deeply, then why would you not provide to those that are looking to learn from you? It's the practical idea of reciprocity. Remember one of our earlier chapters!

Ultimately, I want my audience to leave me saying "*I got it!*" or even better, "*I hope I never have to see you again.*" No, wait, that sounds harsh, but in actuality what they're saying is that I gave them enough to be able to apply what they need, and that makes all the difference to whether I connected with that individual.

Quick story

Did you know that Martin Luther King, Jr. was such a gifted student that he skipped grades 9 and 12 before enrolling at Morehouse College? Although he was the son, grandson and great-grandson of Baptist ministers, King did not intend to follow the family vocation until Morehouse president Benjamin E. Mays, a noted theologian, convinced him otherwise. King was ordained before graduating college with a degree in sociology.

King used his gift and taught us a valuable lesson in thinking strategically without the use of violence to gain equal access to the things that were not equal. The ability to instil courage, empathy and critical thinking in those that followed him allowed his legacy to continue well past his premature death. Your impact should be felt in practice long after your interaction.

In the next chapter, we explore the art of connection. There's a euphoria associated with learning a new thing, especially when you allow yourself to be taught.

7

Be Willing and Open to be Taught

"I have learned that, although I am a good teacher,
I am a much better student, and I was blessed to learn
valuable lessons from my students daily.
They taught me the importance of teaching
to a student - and not to a test." ~ **Erin Gruwell**

Be Willing and Open to be Taught

" Nothing is worse than someone whose ego won't allow them to be taught."

Erin Gruwell (born August 15, 1969) is an American educator known for her unique teaching method, which led to the publication of *The Freedom Writers Diary: How a Teacher and 150 Teens Used Writing to Change Themselves and the World Around Them* (1999).

Erin's teaching philosophy is that of a partnership between student and teacher. She believes firmly that "education is the great equalizer" and credits her ability to listen as the crucial tool which helped her to break down barriers and earn the trust of her students (Granoff, 2009).

The 2007 film, *Freedom Writers*, is based on her story. Gruwell began student teaching in 1994 at Woodrow Wilson High School in Long Beach, California. She was assigned low-performing students in the school, and when only one of the students knew what the Holocaust was, Gruwell changed the theme of her curriculum to "tolerance." Gruwell took the students to see *Schindler's List*, purchased new books out of her own pocket, and scheduled guest speakers.

She also had the students read books written by and about other teenagers in times of war, such as *The Diary of a Young Girl, Zlata's Diary, and Night*. For Erin, the instrument of change is a pen. Faced with divisive classroom politics, prejudice, and violence, students guarded themselves within the armour brought on by gang violence. Writing journals became a solace for many of the students. Because the journals were shared anonymously, teenagers who once refused to speak to someone of a different race became like a family.

In the fall of 1995, Gruwell gave each of her students a bag full of new books and had them make a "toast for change" where she gave each student a plastic champagne glass filled with apple cider, and they all agreed to provide themselves with a second chance at life. After that, she saw a turnaround in them. The students went on to surprise everyone. All 150 Freedom Writers graduated from high school, and many went on to attend college.

Ego trippin'

The United Nations Educational, Scientific and Cultural Organization (UNESCO) published a book entitled *What Makes a Good Teacher?* (1996). Over 500 children aged 8-12 from 50 countries contributed their opinions. One opinion that stood out to me was, "A good teacher is someone who can learn from his students, who can learn with them, and for them. He also must be honest in his relationships with students, and proud enough about his value to work, from there, on helping his students to build their self-esteem."

Now I'd like to bring down portions of this opinion in the next few sections because I don't want anyone to overlook the significance of this message and how it relates to bringing the humanity back into your relationships.

A Good Teacher

Ms. Baker was my third-grade teacher in an elementary school in Brooklyn, NY. While I assume she taught us everything required of her in the 3rd grade, I didn't know much about the school curriculum. I just knew I was required to show up each day, sit in a desk, and remember what Ms. Baker was writing on the chalkboard. It doesn't seem too exciting as I am explaining the setup, but wait. There was something different about how we interacted with Ms. Baker that was different from any of the other teachers I had during that time. Honestly, this was true even through high school.

As a kid, most of my experience in dealing with adults was to shut up, be seen but not heard unless an adult was speaking to you. Some of you may be able to relate to this sentiment. But Ms. Baker didn't necessarily subscribe to that way of thinking. She would encourage us to share things we did over the weekend, explain how we felt about certain current events, share what we thought about what we were learning, open up about our insecurities and fears, and so much more. She wanted us to speak often, and I never recall losing her temper or more impressively, losing control of the class.

Everyone else I learned from would lose it quite often, cuss at us, tell us "*we ain't shit*" or that we would never amount to anything. But Ms. Baker didn't believe in that. She would encourage us to write a summary each day before we ended the class and then share it the next morning. Ms. Baker would share her review as well with us. And in every summary that she shared, she would highlight what she learned new about one of us and how it would help her be a better teacher.

Honesty in Relationships

The next part in that opinion is the emphasis on being "*honest in his relationships.*" I have come to realize that honesty is used far too often in a subjective manner. Someone who claims to be honest in their relationships, yet intentionally omits vital information when sharing a version of the truth, will appear honest. Someone who reveals a portion of the truth and downplays other remnants of the story because it doesn't paint them in a favourable light will also position themselves as honest. The portrayal of honesty can be self-serving when predicated on who's listening, why they're listening, and what I hope for them to remember once they've heard.

Quite frankly, I see some claims of honesty to be pre-meditated, which deters honesty's real purpose.

Honesty is not pre-meditated. It's not a prisoner to the situation. It's not a tool to be used to sway opinion. Honesty is genuine, authentic, and felt, like a way of being regardless of who is watching.

My grandmother would tell me that what you do in the dark when no one is watching is as honest as you'll ever be in this world. I come to embrace that the dark needs to be revered because without the dark, there is no evidence of light.

Those moments of insecurity, self-worth, confidence, fear, courage, love, appreciation, anger, depression, isolation, joy, peace, and contentment are most revealed when no one is watching. Now here's the part that will scare most of you away: honesty in relationships can effortlessly transfer that way of being when no one is watching when everyone is watching without skipping a beat.

When we learn to do this, it's magical in what our relationships transform themselves into. You're no longer controlled by the act of trying to be honest, but rather you are in a state of being where honesty becomes you.

Build their Self-esteem

The last point of emphasis I felt compelled to break down in that opinion:

*"A good teacher is someone who can learn from his students,
who can learn with them, and for them. He also must be honest in
his relationships with students, and proud enough about his value
to work, from there, on helping his students to build their self-esteem."*
is the value in someone else able to "build *their self-esteem.*"

How can you possibly know when someone has a healthy sense
of self-esteem?

Is there a meter found on their forehead that blinks when their
self-esteem is at an acceptable level? Or maybe their hair turns a different color when their self-esteem is getting low.

Think about your oil light or gas meter. I don't recall too many
conversations that I've had with well over 60,000 learners where
they approached me and explicitly stated, "Doc, my self-esteem meter needs some attention. Every time I turn it on, I get a beep alert
indicator stating it needs attention."

Instead of relying on someone's words, I need to study their actions as if no one was watching. Our ability to help others experience small victories daily is critical in establishing a growth mindset
capable of feeling like they can do more and be more.

One of the activities I always implement in every interaction I
have with an audience is describing what they have just heard. Once
they can explain what they just heard, they can begin to tell me how
what they just heard can help them solve a problem. Once they've
described how, they need to say to me when they could implement

the solution to solve the problem. Once they've implemented the solution, how will they know the issue is resolved or simply managed? In other words, what does success look like?

This may seem like a lot, but it rarely takes more than five minutes to get through this type of critical thinking exercise. My goal is to help them visualize what success looks like to them. Not to me, but for them! Understand that helping someone build self-esteem is about assisting them in painting the person that has value for what they need.

Nothing is worse than someone whose ego won't allow them to be taught. For those individuals that believe they know all there is to know about the dynamics of humanity, learning, development, and interaction, then I probably don't have much for you to gravitate toward. Just because we have a title, we're getting paid, or we're being thrust onto centre stage, doesn't mean we've suddenly commanded the right to *not* be taught. If you don't know, there is a thing called group dynamics that happens in every session. Some will settle in and shrink, others will prod some along in thought and discussion, and others will question everything you say, if not verbally then mentally. The point is to learn from every interaction in the room.

Real learning happens symbiotically, and it should not be a top-down approach. You may have the lesson plan, the topic, and the way you want to deliver, but all of that fails if the learner can't provide some insight.

I will confess that I struggled with this one at first, especially after I earned my doctorate. I had spent so much time and money reading, researching, and writing about human dynamics and social behaviour that I felt as if I was ten people all wrapped into one. My level of knowledge grew, but so did my ego. Sometimes barely enough to fit into a room.

I could shut people down quickly with a question into their inquiry. I could dismiss those that I didn't find relevant. Oh yes, it was terrible, but then it all started to turn when one of my attendees at a workshop asked the question, "What do I hope to get out of this while I'm training them?" She flipped the classroom on me, and I had to take a moment to find the right answer that didn't make me sound uninterested. The answer came out like this, "I don't know," and the look on this person's face told me a story that stayed with me all these years.

Her silent story implied that I was just there to pass the time and that I didn't care enough to invest in the opportunity to learn from them. Their opinions didn't matter to me, and I felt they just needed to be here in attendance. None of that narrative felt good, nor was it what I wanted my audience to feel or think as they engaged with me. I wanted them to know that learning is lifelong and infinite. We never stop learning because as Albert Einstein poetically stated, "Once you stop learning, you start dying."

They needed to understand that my position as the facilitator, keynote speaker, author, researcher, and subject matter expert was not all show. Instead, I wanted substance to go along with it. As it turns out, the substance came in the ability to be taught by those I was teaching.

Mindset

This shift in mindset changed the very trajectory of my business practice. Once I became open to the idea of being taught while training, I began to change the design of my curriculum, my interactions, and my plan. I began to implement more opportunities for reflection, discussion, and a flipped-classroom approach. I did more pre-work trying to better understand my audience's needs well in advance of the actual events. I became more inquisitive while training. I elevated my whole way of understanding and found my fulfilment level exponentially better than it had been the prior ten years.

The conversations got better, the feedback became quote-worthy, and most importantly, the audience knew that I cared about their well-being (refer back to an earlier chapter).

All of these "ah-ha" moments were lessons in humanity. It became clear that separating humanity from the craft was a faulty plan that produced an outcome that nobody wanted.

Quick story

Erin Gruwell is a person who wanted to prove the impossible. She declared that she could teach kids who are "unteachable." She inspired kids who wanted to be in gangs and encouraged kids from bad homes to want to learn and read. Ironically enough, Erin Gruwell was planning on becoming a lawyer, but when she watched the Los Angeles riots on TV in the early 1990s, that made her change her mind and life dramatically.

She saw people starting fires, robbing stores, damaging property, and beating up other people because they were angry. Erin believed that she could change how people were reacting to their frustration. She decided to go to work at Woodrow Wilson High School, where the kids were from many different backgrounds, and where she felt she would have a chance to make a difference.

She made a difference not just in what she taught those kids, but more importantly, what she learned about their lives and individual stories—her willingness to be taught allowed everyone's levels of humanity to rise to new heights.

What I believe to be equally significant in this transformation is the much-needed opportunity for personal reflection time.

In the next chapter, we will spend some time understanding what happens when reflection is given equal footing in any interaction you have with an audience of either one or one hundred thousand.

8

Allow Reflection to Happen Organically

Margaret "Meg" Wheatley
Credit image: A New Republic of the Heart

"Without reflection, we go blindly on our way,
creating more unintended consequences,
and failing to achieve
anything useful." ~ **Margaret J. Wheatley**

Allow Reflection to Happen Organically

"I don't want us to settle for an alternative when we can thrive off of the original."

Margaret Wheatley, commonly known as "Meg Wheatley," was born in 1944 and was an American writer and management consultant who studied organizational behaviour. Throughout her professional career, which went by the vague labels of "organizational change," "organizational development," or "management consulting", Meg came upon a realization that if she had an organizational change effort that was successful, it felt like a miracle to her and her company. In other words, she needed to take a step back to better understand the value she brought to a particular project. Without that understanding, neither she nor her company was geared up for success.

The American Society for Training and Development (ASTD) named her one of five living legends. In May 2003, ASTD awarded her their highest honour: "Distinguished Contribution to Workplace Learning and Performance," with the following citation:

> "Meg Wheatley gave the world a new way of thinking about organizations with her revolutionary application of the natural sciences to business management. Her concepts have traveled across national boundaries and through all sectors. Her ideas have found welcome homes in the military, not-for-profit organizations, public schools, and churches as well as in corporations... Through her interdisciplinary curiosity, Meg Wheatley provides new insights into the nature of how people interact and inspires us to

build better organizations and better societies across the globe."

Having success without meaning supplied Meg with very little satisfaction. Her reflection process gave her the time and space to make the type of difference that could only be coined as "legacy" status.

Just be still

Recently, I travelled to Washington, DC in which I took some time to visit several monuments and attractions, such as the Holocaust Museum and the National Museum of African American History and Culture (NMAAHC). While visiting the NMAAHC, I found myself propelled back to a time where life seemed to make more sense. Now, I'm not saying life was easy during these times because the struggle has always been a part of not just my story, but America's story.

However, I felt as if life was simpler and made more sense as I walked through this museum and saw all of the significant influences that helped shape my childhood. Between the music icons, wardrobes, cars, pictures, and quotes, I was given time to reflect on each and remember how prevalent these facets of my life were growing up.

For instance, there was a replica of a jumbo boombox in one of the areas that highlighted musical influences. Now, for those of you too young to know what a boombox is, let me take you on a quick journey. The boombox was a fantastic electronic device with massive

Boombox, 1989, Owned by Gene Siskel and used by Radio Raheem in Spike Lee's movie, Do the Right Thing

speakers, two cassette tape decks for listening and recording, a radio dial, a microphone input, and an equalizer system to control the amount of bass and treble. Although I was never able to afford one, I've used them on many occasions. In fact, I had a small crew in Brooklyn, and we would perform at different parks, dancing to the latest hip-hop sounds and entertaining parkgoers with our moves. We would also compete against other crews that danced as well, something very commonplace during this time as we were during the hip-hop movement.

The boombox revolutionized the enjoyment of listening to music, the recording and dubbing of music, and a person's status in their neighbourhood. If you had one of these back in the day, you were "da man." Shout out to Radio Raheem!

Reflecting on those moments renews my energy. Reflection allows you to experience those times again, while simultaneously learning lessons from the past. When we take time to reflect on a unique event, we are reaffirming the journey in a way that allows us to teach more efficiently.

In *The Alchemist,* written by Paulo Coelho, there is a passage that states, *"Everything that happens once can never happen again. But everything that happens twice will surely happen a third time."* While Coelho argues that every moment is actually designed to only happen once, we want to learn from that moment and not let it slip away. If we don't take the time to learn from it, we run the risk of missing out on the full lesson that should have been discovered. Instead, we settle for an alternative lesson over and over again. I don't want us to settle for an alternative when we can thrive off of the original. This is how I see reflection, but what do some smart people say about this topic?

Sebastian Koole, a professor and author who researches factors associated with reflection, stated, "Reflection on experience is an increasingly critical part of professional development and lifelong learning." (Koole et al., 2011). John Dewey, an American philosopher, psychologist, and educational reformer, wrote, "We do not learn from experience. We learn from reflecting on experience." David Dention, author and educational philosopher, stated,

> *"Reflection is a central feature of experiential education and serves the function of solidifying the connection between what a student experienced and the meaning/learning that they derived from that experience."*

And my favorite passage on the importance of reflection comes from an interview by Samuel Jackson as he talked about his iconic role as Gator in Spike Lee's movie, "Jungle Fever,"

> *"Dance for me, Gator!" Gator was me — I was that character. I'd been out of rehab maybe two weeks when we shot Jungle Fever.*

I didn't need makeup or nothing. In fact, when I showed up to shoot, and I went to craft services to get something to eat, Spike [Lee] had all these Fruit of Islam guys around the set, and they thought I was one of the crackheads from around the neighborhood. They were like, 'Get away from the table!' Gator is really close to me because [he] signified me killing that part of my life and moving on. So when Ossie Davis, the Good Reverend Doctor, killed me in that movie, it kind of freed me from all those demons I had in my real life. That was kind of cool. That was the summer of dueling crackheads. It was me, and Chris Rock was Pookie in New Jack City. Gator was that guy everybody had in their family. I was like, 'This has to be about me ruining my family relationships with all the people that care about me because you get stuff from them, and then you just break their hearts.'

In my experiences, the act of reflection should allow us to simplify our experiences to be in a constant state of learning. As human beings, losing sight of the need for continual reflection seems unrealistic because we should never stop learning from our surroundings, our circumstances, and ourselves.

The misconception is that reflection takes a long time, but the reality is that it can take as short or long as you desire. It's not a matter of quantity; it's pure quality. Yet, without constant reflection, life's lessons can be a bit much for us to digest without feeling overwhelmed. Transferring the complexities of teaching, training, and coaching and prohibiting proper reflection can leave your engagement less than desirable.

Reflection has a variety of intended outcomes, such as creating a greater understanding of self and situation to inform future action. It is also required to develop both a therapeutic relationship and expertise. Knowledge of both the self and the situation has a broader impact on lifelong learning than merely identifying the acquisition of new knowledge and skills.

Effects of reflection

It's a beautiful thing when you aren't tugged in a million different directions, so you have time to think. Due to the sheer quantity of stimuli constantly bombarding us, it can be difficult to grasp everything that you need in a certain amount of time. Quite frankly, most of us are terrible at multitasking, especially when committing something to working memory. So why run the risk of losing your audience?

Moments of reflection are essential for both yourself and your audience. Reflection not only resets the brain, but it re-energizes the brain, which allows us to process what we want to learn. I consider the opportunity to reflect moments of joy.

Joy may be subjective to everyone experiencing it, but it is a fundamental internal construct that is necessary for the soul to flourish. Just like reflection, joy is something that cannot be taken away from you. In other words, it is something you choose to give away. In this case, I choose to give myself and others moments to practice reflection. There is clarity in reflection. There are hard-sought answers in reflection.

We should all strive to better sense and seize those opportunities when they arise. Reflection is a catalyst for change. It's a constant reminder of where you are and where you need to be. It is the ultimate elixir for real learning.

Take a moment to think about the effect that reflection has on our brain chemistry. Reflection allows us to reward ourselves for intentionally taking action to fix a mistake or to contemplate on how something can be used to make something else better. The opportunity to make something better or to correct a mistake is part of the reward. When our brain senses a reward is about to happen, it produces a chemical called dopamine. There are tons of research on the impact of dopamine on our moods, our desires, our cravings, among other things. However, the most significant benefit of dopamine production is that it causes us to act.

Think about how much more powerful you become when allowed to reflect, reward, and ultimately, take action. You've just opened up a portal for increased intellectual capacity and acceptance for learning to take place.

One time, I had an attendee at a workshop of mine actually tell me that he was never given an opportunity in any kind of continuing education or training where he could just sit still and reflect. I gave him and all the attendees in a standing-room-only workshop just that. He went on to say that his mind was so much more accepting of the lesson and topics on that day's agenda.

This is something you can work strategically into your sessions, but not just in a structured and formal manner. It's vital to keep in mind that reflection happens best when it happens organically.

Inspiration happens when least expected

Think about a time when you said something so profound that it made you stop for a moment and think. Maybe you even wrote this thought down. If it was that profound to you as the facilitator, then why not give your audience the same courtesy of allowing that profound moment to sink deeper into their lives as well? Extraordinary moments are sometimes lightning in a bottle. They're rare and unique, but when they happen, that occurrence should not be taken lightly. Inspiration in and of itself I consider to be a foolish novelty if it is not directed at making something or someone else better.

The Collins dictionary defines inspiration as *"a feeling of enthusiasm you get from someone or something, that gives you new and creative ideas."* What better way to empower your audience than providing them with the space to create new ideas? Now that's powerful!

Quick story

Since 1966, Margaret Wheatley has worked globally in many different roles: a speaker, teacher, community worker, consultant, advisor, formal leader. From these deep and varied experiences, she has defined and shared the unshakable conviction that leaders must learn how to evoke people's inherent generosity, creativity, and need for community. Meg's keystone contribution to reflection is her "Warrior" training, which is training for the human spirit to be the presence of insight and compassion.

In my experiences, insight and compassion have been a direct derivative of personal reflection. It is essential to know the difference between the two words because each word warrants its own spirit or behaviour. Insight from reflection allows us to better comprehend the inner nature of things. It gives us a perspective that generally gets overlooked from the surface. The behaviour insight drives our curiosity. Compassion not only provides perspective, but it leads to deeper connections on a physiological plane where we become in tuned to others pain. The behaviour compassion elicits is service. Meg combined all the elements required to build a wholistic environment where the ability to learn, be taught and teach back to others became the foundation for her sustained success in building relationships.

In the next chapter, I want us to be more intentional in how we think about the consequences that matter most to us, and our audience. Beneath the surface, there should be a common thread that binds us together, but it takes effort to get there.

9

Be Driven by The Outcomes That Matter Most

Obama Prayer
Image credit: unknown

"Now, as a nation, we don't promise equal

outcomes, but we were founded on the idea
everybody should have an equal opportunity to
succeed. No matter who you are, what you look
like, where you come from, you can make it.
That's an essential promise of America.
Where you start should not determine where you end up." ~ **Barack**
Obama

Be Driven by The Outcomes That Matter Most

"When there is a plan or goal you want to achieve, and it involves
something bigger than yourself, I believe it requires precise calculations to
measure your progress."

I grew to appreciate President Barack Obama the more I got to
know his story. Over his eight years, he did his best with the challenging situation left for him by the Bush Administration. If you
read anything about his background, you've probably read that after high school, Obama studied at Occidental College in Los Angeles
for two years. He then transferred to Columbia University in New
York City, graduating in 1983 with a political science degree. After working in the business sector for two years, Obama moved to
Chicago in 1985.

There, he worked on the impoverished south side as a community organizer for low-income residents in the Roseland and Altgeld
Gardens communities. In his speech announcing his candidacy for
president of the United States, Obama would note that these communities provided him with " the best education I ever had."

I often wonder if Mr. Obama dreamed of his dramatic rise to the presidency. Did he visualize specific outcomes for his life, and if he did, what steps did he take along the way to ensure he was meeting those expectations?

Remember what?

Dreams are, and sometimes can be, utterly indescribable. They make no sense at times. There doesn't seem to be a rhyme or reason for some of the dreams that we have. However, there are times where our dreams are as crystal clear as if we were viewing them from a clear glass window. It's in those moments we tell ourselves to write them down, investigate them further, make some sense of them, and then take action. Yup, that's what we say but, in those moments when it's time to write them down, we lose specific details about the dream. We struggle to remember the exact sequence of things that happened.

It may have been the perfect set of words in the dream, but when faced with the act of recreating that sense or feeling, we typically fall short. We're left to interpret as best we can what took place in the dream. Now it's a matter of whether what we wrote down or what we recollect is actually what happened. It can be an endless cycle of mental anguish because we want to get the vision exactly as it played out.

Here I am standing at a door that won't open. It's dark outside, but I can see a slight hint of movement through the darkness. The next thing you know, I am asked to find two dancers from Africa who have become very popular on social media. In looking for these dancers, I get reminded that I need to finish building the boat that will take me to Italy. Once I get to Italy, there is a shepherd that will bring me a silver tray. What in the "*Sam Hill*" is happening? Now if you can decipher what any of this means, feel free to let me know. I'm sure there were more details to this dream that could have provided logical sense to its interpretation, but this is what I remember.

Regardless if you believe you dream or not, researchers have found that people usually have several dreams a night, each one typically lasting between 5 to 20 minutes. As much as 95 percent of all dreams are quickly forgotten shortly after waking. According to one theory about why dreams are so difficult to remember, it is believed that the changes in the brain which occur during sleep do not support the information processing and storage needed for memory formation to take place. If on average, I only remember roughly five percent of the dream, then maybe what I'm writing down and remembering are the essential parts of the dream. Cause for further investigation!

I've read that dreams are God's messages, but I will leave that up to you as to how you interpret the meaning of dreams. I segued into dreams because I made the initial statement and inquiry regarding Barack Obama. Did he dream of his meteoric rise to the presidency? Did he visualize specific outcomes for his life, and if he did, what steps did he take along the way to ensure he was meeting those expectations?

When there is a plan or goal you want to achieve, and it involves something bigger than yourself, I believe it requires precise calculations to measure your progress. There will be many things you want to accomplish in a set amount of time. But ask yourself, if my audience could only retain ten percent of what I teach them, what would I want that 10 percent to be? If you don't know the answer, ask your audience! It's that simple.

Your audience is your client, customer, confidant, lover, friend, or foe. So there needs to be an intentional emphasis placed on their needs that at times may differ from your plan. I like to refer to it as outcomes, and they matter to your audience of either 5000 participants or just 1.

The Misinterpretation of Outcomes

We can all admit that we get angry. If you haven't gotten angry so far in your life, just keep on living. It's going to happen. But in those moments of anger, I find that there's a tendency to misdiagnose why we're angry in the first place. Sure, on the surface, something may appear to have triggered that reaction. But more than likely, the angry outburst didn't happen because of the most immediate event. That cue to be mad happened a long time ago, and we associated it with the circumstance that just happened.

The truth of the matter is this: if you take a more in-depth look into the issue, you may find that you're not suffering from anger but something more defined, such as lack of patience. Take a moment to think about how you feel after the anger has subsided. You begin to backtrack to all of the events that led up to the angry outburst. Could you have exhibited more patience, in the beginning, to prevent the anger from happening? What about anxiety?

If we're anxious about something and we want it to happen or not happen so badly, anything could be the trigger for an angry outburst.

The point is looking on the surface of things can be misleading to what truly needs to be measured and investigated further. There's an old proverb that I'm paraphrasing: "You shouldn't just treat the symptoms but rather treat the root cause for true healing to take place." Treating the symptoms is just a temporary fix, but it won't prevent the situation from happening again. Addressing the root cause of something teaches us a whole new meaning.

As I dive a bit deeper into this subject of outcomes, I want us to think deeper and reflect on what actually matters to our audience. Are we too concerned with the surface level symptoms, or should we teach, coach, and guide those to the root cause?

Outcomes Matter

Knowing what outcomes matter to your audience provides a clearer vision or roadmap to what will be accomplished when we engage with one another. It not only provides a shared understanding, but it also encourages confidence to build together with the knowledge that your audience will be equipped to do more after an engagement. I will explain more in a bit.

For all of my academic people, you may think that outcomes are interchangeable with learning objectives, but the two are quite contrary. Defining outcomes can take our audience through a progression of behaviours intended to help them progress to higher levels of personal and professional achievement. It's not predicated solely on whether someone passes the grade, but more on incorporating specific behaviours that help them better prepare for what success looks like. It's about putting practice to application so that your audience feels engaged and equipped with the proper growth mindset to do more and learn more.

It is the ultimate end goal: to win the game. (You can define your own game, scenario, or situation to the metaphor of wining and finding success.) The distinction between learning objectives and what I just described lies within what students actually know and what they can do as a result of their time in school. More on objectives in a moment.

As I mentioned previously, think about outcomes as the behaviours you want your learners to exhibit as a result of interacting with your lesson, training, workshop, etc. But then ask, are those outcomes aligned with the outcomes that my participants need? If we're not careful, there will be a disconnect.

Now, back to learning objectives. Objectives are what is designed to be discovered during the lesson. For example, in a math course, you learn to add 1+1. That is the objective which is taught for that particular lesson. In an outcome, you want your learners to use that knowledge gained from the objective and put it in good practice where it becomes useful to them.

Think back to an earlier chapter, where I noted that learners don't want to just show up anymore. The education experience has to be dynamic, in which learning has to lead to an immediate ability to do something more. If we're not making sure our learners can do more when they engage with us, then we've missed out on a tremendous opportunity. So back to outcomes—the outcomes that matter most should relate to three key areas: timeliness, achievement, and progression.

Timeliness

When a learner interacts with me, the event, the lesson, or the learning platform, I need to help them think critically about how they can do something better and more efficiently. They need to feel confident that what they are being shown leads to better performance and better understanding. I am instilling in them behaviours of measurable practice intended to lead to successful outcomes as they apply it to their lives. Theory and concept are elegant, but practical application to support theory and concept is even better.

With timeliness comes that feeling of completeness. Having successfully completed a task rewards our confidence affirms good habits and leads to a growth mindset. If I want learners to master a specific skill so that they become more efficient, then I need to ensure that my outcomes align to that particular value. I am going to design my engagement to do just that. In the end, your audience will be able to speak for you. They can be your biggest supporters if you focus on this particular outcome.

Achievement

This helps your audience move from one place of understanding to a different, more improved place of understanding. Yes, I may now know why 1+1 = 2, but I can now apply it, which allows me to accomplish a particular goal. In other words, I need to help my audience feel like what they've learned leads somewhere, and it's not just for the sake of knowing. Every outcome promotes action for the learner. It supports behavioural shifts in habit and mindset.

Progression

This is the ultimate outcome that will matter most to your audience. This outcome takes him to another level of opportunity. It exposes him to new doors to be opened because of his new ability, habits, and mindset. He just invested time with you, and he wants to feel like it was worth their time. Not only did they show up, but they can now show out. This simply means they want to show competency to others, they to a potential employer, to their existing boss, or to just brag to their friends for their self-efficacy.

That's the power of outcomes, especially in these three areas.

Quick story

Obama arrived as a 23-year-old Columbia University graduate in Roseland in the summer of 1985 to embark on a quest for a sense of purpose and belonging. It was a confusing, conflicting time to be black in Chicago. The election two years earlier of Harold Washington, the city's first African American mayor, energized black residents. However, many of them were still living in poverty, and entire sections of black Chicago seemed to be turning into war zones.

The dispatches that journalists like Alex Kotlowitz and Nicholas Lemann filed from the city's gigantic high-rise housing projects during Obama's time in the city are shocking even today. In essence, children were crawling on the ground to avoid bullets, apartments firebombed, and a prolonged gun battle between gangs in two neighbouring high-rise buildings that drew not a single police car in response.

As Obama's time on the south side progressed, he grew preoccupied with the fate of Roseland's young people, especially the teenage boys, who seemed increasingly lost and hopeless. It was not just money they were lacking, he realized, but something deeper. "When I'm president," Obama said, "the first part of my plan to combat urban poverty will be to replicate the Harlem Children's Zone in 20 cities across the country." With a candor unusual for a presidential candidate, Obama acknowledged the high price of his program: "Now how much will this cost?" he asked. "I'll be honest, it can't be done on the cheap."

President Obama understood that focusing on the wrong outcomes would only be a band-aid solution to the much deeper, systemic open wound. Instead, he rallied his message around the most relevant results that mattered to that community. Was his work perfectly executed? Not in the slightest. But the awareness, heightened conversation, and resources needed to combat the level of poverty experienced in that community was the type of focus targeted at the right outcomes that mattered most.

I've come to believe through experience that our most significant level of growth happens when we are most uncomfortable. I want to explore that a bit further in the next chapter and how working through uncomfortable circumstances produces courage, strength, and a heightened level of self-awareness needed to bring humanity back to our relationships.

10

Get Comfortable Making Learning Uncomfortable

Aston Kutcher
Credit image: unknown

"I don't believe that old cliché that good things come to those who wait. I think good things come to those who want something so bad they can't sit still." ~ Ashton Kutcher

Get Comfortable Making Learning Uncomfortable

"Routines may make you feel at ease and in control, but what a constant routine really does is dull your sensitivities."

If you're familiar with the actor Ashton Kutcher, you've probably grown to appreciate his growth as an actor, activist, father, and husband. He is blazing trails, taking risks, and living the life of uncomfortable experiences to help him grow mentally, physically, and spiritually. The model turned actor is the physical embodiment of what 'fun' is supposed to look like. He was adored as the brainless yet lovable Michael Kelso in "That '70s Show," and I enjoyed him as the flawed yet brilliant Steve Jobs in the 2013 biopic, "Jobs."

Nevertheless, Ashton's journey to fame is quite remarkable and has had more than its fair share of thorns and roses alike. But it was in his foray into the world of entrepreneurship that the world was treated to a new side of the Hollywood superstar.

Ashton, on many occasions, has publicly spoken about how being a successful entrepreneur entails the need for a creative idea, the will to work on that idea, and a lingering element of surprise so that you can wow every individual when you finally make it big. It is this lingering element of surprise, which continually reminds him of the need to be comfortable in the uncomfortable.

So What, I'm Comfortable!

I was amongst 35 or so boys standing in a straight, carefully guarded line. I was probably around 9 or 10 years old. We had just finished our morning lesson, and as usual, every Wednesday we went to the cathedral for prayer and communion.

My Catholic schooling was a bizarre experience, as I never really understood religion, religious protocols, the concept of heaven and hell, or even Jesus Christ. This isn't to say I was uninterested in the experience – I simply wanted to understand it better. However, no one had ever really taken the time to teach me about religion or the role it should play in my life. Although it was my mother who enrolled me in this parochial school, she never explained religion to me either. I never did ask why she enrolled me here, but I'm led to believe she simply did not like the public school down the block from our apartment in Brooklyn. Instead, I took two trains and a bus to get to this place.

Nevertheless, this brick ironclad structure with its gated concrete playground, cinderblock walls, cold floors, dim halls, bright classrooms, and wooden chairs was filled with screaming kids, flying nuns, and 36-inch yardsticks. These nuns weren't shy about using them on us and had a terrifying presence wherever they went. Although they wore these brown, hard-bottom shoes, they always managed to sneak up on you when you least expected it.

We also had to wear uniforms, a very stylish combination of grey, burgundy, and plaid. I'm sure there are some of you out there reading this that know exactly what I mean by the uniforms.

In terms of my classmates, they were a mix of lower-class black, Caribbean, Puerto Rican, and Italian We were an unruly bunch of misfits, but we didn't see or understand race because we were all poor. We had that in common, and that alone was enough to make us act out. Usually, we acted out against the overwhelming oppression that we felt coming from the school's authority. In short, we were comfortable being uncomfortable with them.

So here we were, standing in this line on a typical Wednesday. As the priest said a few words regarding Jesus Christ dying for our sins and rising from the dead, we all stood silently and recited prayers we were told to say. One by one, each boy would kneel in front of the altar, hold out his hands, and receive a communion cracker. Well, on that typical Wednesday, when it was my turn, I decided that I was no longer comfortable kneeling before this man and receiving this ritual of response. Mind you, I had participated in this solemn ceremony for about two or three months. I just didn't understand why I was doing this or what it meant for me in this school.

I stood defiant in front of the church, the nuns, and God, for all I knew. "Father" as he was referenced, attempted to push me down to my knees by my shoulders. He failed! The nuns were up next. They used the yardsticks on my legs to get my knees to buckle. They failed! The other kids began to rally behind me, but that didn't last long. Did I mention how terrifying these nuns were? I was on an island representing something that I could not describe. It was uncomfortable, but I remained comfortable in my position.

After the incident, I received any form of punishment that they could manifest. I got twenty or so whacks from the yardstick. I had to hold books in either hand out to my side for hours in front of the classroom. I had to stand in the corner wearing a dunce cap on my head. I had to clean the boy's bathroom, and I had to write on the chalkboard, "I will not disrupt communion again" one hundred times.

All of this for wanting to understand why I was being forced to do something I didn't understand. Think about this for a moment. How many times have you just gone with the flow of something for fear that you would be uncomfortable not going with the flow? How did it help you grow? Learn?

I am a firm believer that real learning happens when one is uncomfortable. Routines may make you feel at ease and in control, but what a constant routine really does is dull your sensitivities.

Real learning happens when one is forced to decide between choices, and neither option seems to be the right answer.

Seth Godin, an American author and former dot com business executive, stated, "*Discomfort brings engagement and change. Discomfort means you're doing something others are unlikely to do because they're hiding out in the comfortable zone.*" Being uncomfortable also requires a higher level of honesty and transparency. Something Seth also said that resonates with me is, "*In a crowded marketplace, fitting in is a failure. In a busy marketplace, not standing out is the same as being invisible.*"

Some of our most endearing polarizing individuals in life, whether good or bad, are those people whose lives we can peer into. We find comfort in knowing the struggle of others, especially those we admire, celebrate, or just feel empathy towards.

As an individual in the training and development space, the level of transparency I exhibit humanizes me when I am in front of an audience. The stories you share with your audience and the insight you provide is meant to foster a deeper connection with those who are listening and engaging with you.

This meaningful engagement factor drives impact for you and, most importantly, your attendees. Another essential aspect of being transparent is the solicitation of emotions. Face it; most people don't like to deal with their emotions, especially in a setting where others are watching. But that's where you come in. I always want to tell people at the beginning of one of my speeches, lectures, training sessions, or coaching opportunities, that what I say may make you feel a bit uncomfortable. In other words, I'm going to challenge you to tackle your biases, beliefs, and experiences from new perspectives to contribute to how and what you learn. I am helping my audience grow as individuals, and I take that as a personal responsibility.

Survival Instincts

Take a moment to think about what happens when we sense an uncomfortable situation. Our brains are programmed with the survival instinct of fight or flight. Our stress levels spike, our body temperature rises, and our hands get a little sweaty. So many things are happening in that precise moment. Some of us go into problem-solving mode, some of us go into panic mode. There's a continuum of instincts that cause us to fight or flee.

Harvard Health Publishing labels it as a survival mechanism, enabling people and other mammals to react quickly to life-threatening situations.

Now let me be clear: we're talking about being uncomfortable in the classroom, auditorium, workshop, seminar, family dinner, etc. In other words, we're in a controlled environment, albeit I bet what I'm about to say can and does work in uncontrolled environments.

Nonetheless, when we feel this way, wonderful chemicals in the brain called adrenaline and glutamate are produced. Our body releases these chemicals in preparation for dealing with a potentially harmful or undesired situation. They cause our senses to be heightened, our hearts to race, and our bodies to sweat. But let's dive a bit deeper into this because as a person engaging with other human beings or even as just one person talking to another, it helps to understand why certain things happen. Not only that, when we can better understand how to recognize what's happening, we can adjust as needed.

Brain chemistry

Each time the brain produces certain chemicals, scientists believe it expands our comfort level even if you don't know that is what's happening. As adrenaline and glutamate get produced, shortly after that comes dopamine, simply telling your body that it's not as scary as we thought it would be. Now dopamine production allows you to feel comfort and experience relief because you just got past an area in which you were uncomfortable. Most leaders engage in certain behaviours that quite literally affect their own brain chemistry and that of their followers, such as exhibiting empathy and becoming attuned to others' moods. (Goleman and Boyatzis, 2008).

Each time you achieve comfort and confidence with your audience, the more you can expand your agenda. Researchers have also labelled this "social circuitry." The only way to develop your social circuitry effectively is to undertake the hard work of changing your behaviour (see "Primal Leadership: The Hidden Driver of Great Performance," our December 2001 HBR article with Annie McKee). Ultimately, the goal is to help your audience do more, be more, learn more, and engage more.

You do that by creating an environment where the brain is free and pushed to expand, grow, and expand again. You can do this as much as you need but always build in reflection so you can adequately gauge where your people are. I hope by now that you've noticed a trend in how everything has a relationship to something else within the book.

Quick story

"I had $100 and was in a two-bedroom apartment with five other guys in Hell's Kitchen, and I remember very vividly that it was terrifying," reflected Kutcher. By this time, Kutcher had modelled for brands such as Calvin Klein before landing Michael Kelso's role on "That '70s Show." He had a boy scout sleeping bag and was sleeping on a futon watching roaches crawl across the floor.

The story is that he would walk 50 blocks down the road to his modelling agency every day and sit on their couch for eight hours a day, waiting for them to send him out. This made the agency uncomfortable, but he would sit there and wait. They would ask him what he was doing and why he would just sit there, and his response was simple: "This is my job, so I'll be here until you're ready to send me out." They got so annoyed with him, they'd just send him out to everything.

Getting comfortable with the uncomfortable requires a willingness from us, as individuals, to enter a "program" of change. I learned to develop a personal vision for change, and then I underwent a thorough diagnostic assessment, akin to a medical checkup, to identify areas of social weakness and strength. The results were a whole lotta insecurity, fear, worry, and false bravado. I discovered these force fields that I used to protect me, or at least what I perceived as protection. The thing about force fields is that they serve two purposes; to keep things out and to keep things in.

I realized that growth could never happen for me as I claimed I wanted and needed if I continued to rely on this barrier of protection. It wasn't really protection at all. It was all a ruse! I decided to destroy the elements that kept the force field in place so that it was permanently weakened—a scary proposition to say the least. There I was, open and accessible. Vulnerable to all of the vices that could disrupt and destroy my purpose. I was terrified but never felt freer in my life.

Bring it on haters! Bring it on doubters! Bring everything you've got that is meant to derail me. I needed to feel it all and stop pretending. That's being uncomfortable, and that is where I find myself today. No longer afraid to be present. No longer worried about what may or may not come but taking each interaction with another human being as an opportunity to learn.

Your level of impact will depend on how willing you are to become uncomfortable. So whether you're having a conversation with a group of strangers or just having dinner with the family, remember that learning happens at every interaction, and you can help others, and yourself be better prepared.

I feel pretty sure, of course I'm open for debate, that nothing happens by default but by design. We can manifest what we want, not just from our words' power but in alignment with our actions. Actions require intent, effort, and continuity. If you ever want to get really good at something, you practice, right? In the final bonus chapter, I want us to understand this principle's significance, which is true regardless of circumstances. Practice.

11

Practice, Rinse, Repeat

Maya Angelou
Credit image: unknown

"One isn't necessarily born with courage, but one
is born with potential. Without courage, we cannot
practice any other virtue with consistency.
We can't be kind, true, merciful, generous, or honest." ~ Maya
Angelou

Practice, Rinse, Repeat

"Now the train was where I needed it to be the whole time, but simply watching it didn't get me any closer to catching it."

Maya Angelou is widely known as a voice for women, especially black women, and her works have courageously covered themes of identity, racism, and family. During an interview with "USA Today" in 1988, Angelou said, "One isn't necessarily born with courage, but one is born with potential. Without courage, we cannot practice any other virtue with consistency." As you may expect, Angelou's creative genius didn't expose itself without hard work. She was a true master of habits, routines, and consistency. Here's how she described her writing habits in a 1983 interview with Claudia Tate (as covered in Mason Currey's book Daily Rituals),

"I usually get up at about 5:30, and I'm ready to have coffee by 6, usually with my husband. He goes off to his work around 6:30, and I go off to mine. I keep a hotel room in which I do my work—a tiny, mean room with just a bed, and sometimes if I can find it, a face basin. I keep a dictionary, a Bible, a deck of cards and a bottle of sherry in the room. I try to get there around 7, and I work until 2 in the afternoon. If the work is going badly, I stay until 12:30. If it's going well, I'll stay as long as it's going well. It's lonely, and it's marvelous. I edit while I'm working. When I come home at 2, I read over what I've written that day, and then try to put it out of my mind. I shower, prepare dinner so that when my husband comes home, I'm not totally absorbed in my work. We have a semblance of a normal life. We have a drink together and have dinner. Maybe after dinner, I'll read to him what I've written that day. He doesn't comment. I don't invite comments from anyone but my editor, but hearing it aloud is good. Sometimes I hear the dissonance; then I try to straighten it out in the morning."

Angelou's routine and her willingness to sit down and do the work for at least five hours each day — even when it was going poorly — is just another reminder that great artists don't wait for inspiration to strike.

Atomic Habits

If you've been around me for any length of time, you may have quickly realized that there are some common phrases I choose to use repeatedly. "Let's be clear" is one of them. "Let me make sure I understand" happens to be another one. And one of my favourites, "Some people like the pickle better cucumber," is one I might have to explain better another time. But one I've just started to put into rotation is, "Freedom has its privileges, but order comes with a purpose."

Good habits become engrained in your daily routine the more you practice. There is an order to things that makes for good outcomes. Repetition is the key, not the number of days you try something. If I practice to the point where I develop a good lather (i.e. sweat), I am simultaneously developing a higher level of confidence, especially for my craft. I'm doing my audience a better service because I'm letting them know that I value their time. Why? I didn't just show up because it was my job or because I received a speaking fee. I'm here prepared, ready to learn, prepared to participate, ready to grow.

I recall having a vision one morning regarding a commuter train. Now in this vision, I watched the train gain speed, only to suddenly realize that if I didn't stop watching it and start moving in its direction, I would not be able to catch it. Well, guess what? I was not able to catch it at the stop I was supposed to, only to find it later in the vision. Now the train was where I needed it to be the whole time, but simply watching it didn't get me any closer to catching it. I had to start moving toward it before I knew it would be coming so that when it actually came to the station, I was prepared to board. "All aboard, tickets please."

My practice is my purpose. It is what I chose to do. I decided to empower and inspire the lives of learners. You're reading this because maybe you chose the same path. Perhaps it's not in the classroom. Maybe it's behind the pulpit, perhaps it's on the playground, or perhaps it's at your job. It doesn't really matter where the location is; what matters is why you do it.

To become better, possibly even great at something, you have to try things that may be unconventional to some, and that's okay! Even though learning and development have to evolve, many professionals and non-professionals haven't been willing to evolve. The same is valid for humanity.

As a society, long lost are the days where we were actually bored. In other words, there is an artificial stimulus available to you at the blink of an eye. All of it is happening, but is any of it important when it comes to helping us learn more, be more, and do more? I take personal responsibility for the lives that I impact because there's so much noise available to us. At least when my audience interacts with all ten of me, they will have the time to mitigate the noise, focus on what's important to them, and build their lives the way they envisioned.

Quick story

No music, no calls, and a bottle of sherry in empty hotel rooms described the creative writing process of the legendary Maya Angelou. She was strict about her writing conditions and notorious for craving alone time to think, so much so that she wrote in near-empty hotel rooms, with no art on the walls to distract her. This level of practice, rinse, and repeat led her to produce six volumes of an autobiography and six books of poetry that catapulted her to the national stage in 1993 when she read "On the Pulse of Morning" at the 42nd presidential inauguration of Bill Clinton.

I've yet to find the level of discipline that Ms. Angelou exhibited, but what I have found is the significance of doing my work with great enthusiasm, passion, and care for others. Whenever I engage with an individual, I prepare and walk into that interaction to learn from and with that person. The beautiful thing about it is that it's never scripted so that my mannerisms or responses are chambered, cocked, and ready to be fired. No, each interaction is unique and designed to happen just once. Even if you're speaking to the same person or group of people over some time, each time has to be treated as a new engagement, so we don't take for granted the significance of each encounter.

After so many years of being in my profession, I've found that it takes more effort than you ever thought you would need to provide. It requires a high level of preparation, consistency, and practice, all to prepare you for that next encounter. Your life's work depends on your ability to be open to life's lessons that every engagement provides. We grow from our shortcomings, whether we realize it or not. Our mistakes are the perfect teacher.

My grandmother would say that "*I've got good soil, and you've got to decide what you're going to plant.*" My reaction, "*What, Grams?*" I would mutter under my breath, "I'm not a farmer." But the larger metaphor was on point.

In our unique professions, we all bring good soil, but it's a matter of choice as to what seeds we're willing to sow. If we only sow seeds of "I" or "me," then we run the risk of harvesting a crop only sustainable to feed for a couple of seasons. But if we sow seeds of "us" and "we," then we've harvested a crop incapable of experiencing drought. Each time you inspire more than just yourself, you create a trickle-down effect that will shower others to help their harvest grow. It matters how you learn!

TYING IT ALL TOGETHER

There is a golden thread or universal language that binds our humanity to one another. Yet, in many of our professions, those principles have been neglected. I say that's where we've got it all wrong.

Tying a knot
Image credit: unknown

Our work, our identity, and our purpose often gets consumed by the task-oriented work that we do. In those tasks, we lose sight of the larger meaning. In my experiences, my audience of 1 or 100,000 could always tell. These perspectives that I mention throughout the book are parts of your persona. When they work in accord with one another, the impact you make with your audience will shine most.

There must be an awareness of their presence within you because that's how you know they're working as they should. It's not about multiple personalities or anything related to schizophrenic behaviour. It's about embracing what we as humans need to establish a connection with one another. We need to reinject authenticity into our ways, our work, our daily living. It's a battle played between what we need and what a new normal should feel like in a 24/7 connected world.

There is not a moment in time where a person can be bored anymore.

Nevertheless, I want you to take these perspectives into mind, and determine what they mean to you and how you can best position them in your profession. For me, it's a matter of helping people think for themselves. For you, it may be different. Regardless of your business, you can connect with your audience on a whole new level. I bet your audience is waiting for you. Get there!

CHAPTER RESOURCES

This section has included a detailed list of notes, references, and citations for each chapter in the book. I trust that most readers will find this list to be sufficient. However, I also realize that scientific literature changes over time and the references for this book may need to be updated. Furthermore, I fully expect that I made a mistake somewhere in this book - either attributing an idea to the wrong person or not giving credit to someone where it is due. If you believe this to be the case, please email me at sbailey@bcg-northamerica.com to fix the issue as soon as possible.

CHAPTER RESOURCES

Chapter 1

Aristotle, 384-322 BC

George, B. (2007). True north: Discover your authentic leadership. Jossey-Bass. San Francisco, CA.

Miller, A. (2008). The Drama of the Gifted Child: The Search for the True Self, Third Edition. Basic Books. New York, NY.

Chapter 2

Csikszentmihalyi, M. (1975). Beyond boredom and anxiety. San Francisco, Jossey-Bass.

Ducksters. (2021). Biography: Eleanor Roosevelt for Kids. *Ducksters.*

Ekko, E. (2015), 10 Things You Didn't Know About Eleanor Roosevelt.

Eleanor Roosevelt (November 2009). History. A&E Television Networks.

Holbeche, L. and Springett, N. (2003) In Search of Meaning in the Workplace.
   Horsham, Roffey Park.

Kahn, W.A. (1990) Psychological conditions of personal engagement and disengagement at work, Academy of Management Journal, Vol 33, pp692-724.

Maslach, C. Schaufelli, W.B. and Leiter, M.P. (2001) 'Job burnout', Annual Review of Psychology, Vol 52, pp397-422.

Saks, A.M. (2006) Antecedents and consequences of employee engagement, Journal of Managerial Psychology, Vol 21, No 6, pp600-619.

Chapter 3

Bibliomotion (2013) Conversational Intelligence: How Great Leaders Build Trust and Get Extraordinary Results. The Caring Effect.

Carmon, I., Knizhnik, S. (2015). Notorious RBG: The Life and Times of Ruth Bader Ginsburg. New York, NY: HarperCollins Publishers.

Glaser, J.E. (2017). Celebrate and reward good efforts. Psychology Today.

Chapter 4

Cadeiro-Kaplan, K. (2002). Literacy ideologies: Critically engaging the language arts curriculum. Language Arts, 79, 372–381.

Comber, B. (2001). Classroom explorations in critical literacy.

Frye, N. (2008). Words with Power: Being a Second Study of the Bible and Literature. Vol 26. University of Toronto Press: Toronto.

Gooch, B. (2017). Rumi's Secret: The Life of the Sufi Poet of Love. New York, NY: HarperCollins Publishers.

In H. Fehring & P. Green (Eds.), Critical literacy: A collection of articles from the Australian Literacy Educators' Association (pp. 90–102). Newark, DE: International Reading Association.

Janks, H. (2000). Domination, access, diversity, and design: A synthesis for critical literacy education. Educational Review, 52, 175–186.

Chapter 5

Burchfield, C. M., & Sappington, J. (1999). Participation in classroom discussion. Teaching of Psychology, 26, 290291. (ES)

Cohen, M. (1991). Making class participation a reality. PS: Political Science & Politics, 24, 699703. (IT)

Dancer, D., & Kamvounias, P. (2005). Student involvement in assessment: A project designed to assess class participation fairly and reliably. Assessment & Evaluation in Higher Education, 30, 445454. (ES)

Junn, E. (1994). Pearls of wisdom: Enhancing student class participation with an innovative exercise. Journal of Instructional Psychology, 21, 385387. (ES)

Smith, D. G. (1977). College classroom interactions and critical thinking. Journal of Educational Psychology, 69, 180190. (ES)

Weaver, R. R., & Qi, J. (2005). Classroom organization and participation: College students' perceptions. The Journal of Higher Education, 76, 570601. (ES)

Chapter 6

Bandura, A. (1994). Self-efficacy. In V. S. Ramachaudran (Ed.), Encyclopedia of human behavior (Vol. 4, pp. 71-81). New York: Academic Press. (Reprinted in H. Friedman [Ed.], Encyclopedia of mental health. San Diego: Academic Press, 1998).

Friedman [Ed.], Encyclopedia of mental health. San Diego: Academic Press, 1998.

Yarber et al. (2015), Evaluating a train-the-trainer approach for improving capacity for evidence-based decision making in public health. BMC Health Services Research.

Chapter 7

Freedom Writers., & Gruwell, E. (1999). The Freedom Writers diary: how a teacher and 150 teens used writing to change themselves and the world around them. New York: Doubleday.

UNESCO. (1996). What makes a Good Teacher?

Chapter 8

Koole et al. (2011). Factors confounding the assessment of reflection: a critical review. BMC Medication Education.

Sandars, J. (2009). The use of reflection in medical education: AMEE Guide No. 44. Medical Teacher Journal. The University of Leeds, UK 2009; 31: 685–695.

Sebastiaan Koole, Tim Dornan, Leen Aper, Albert Scherpbier, Martin Valcke, Janke Cohen-Schotanus and Anselme Derese.

Chapter 9

Bax, N., Lawson, M., Newbie, D., Stark, D. (2005). Developing an outcome-focused core curriculum.

Grant, J. (2018). Principles of Curriculum Design, Understanding Medical Education, (71-88).

Chapter 10

(2004). That '70s show: the age of pluralism in Chicago; The artist as collector. [Munster, Ind.]: Northern Indiana Arts Association.

Boyatzis, R., Goleman, D. (2008). Social Intelligence and the Biology of Leadership. Harvard Business Review.

Boyatzis, R., Goleman, D., McKee, A. (2001). Primal Leadership: The Hidden Driver of Great Performance. Harvard Business Review.

Bonus Chapter

Biography.com Editors. (2014). Maya Angelou Biography. The Biography.com website.

CONCLUSION

There were these bland tannish-coloured square tiles that covered the floor from end to end. I remember counting the number of specs each tile had on its pale, dusty surface. I think I may have counted almost 10,000 specs as I waited anxiously for my name to be called. I, along with several other people, sat in these blue plastic-back chairs with the chrome metal base that slid just a little each time you adjusted yourself. I was educated, full of talent, full of ideas, fashionable, insightful, and charming. On the surface, some would say I had it all together. I drove a nice vehicle, and I always presented myself with an impeccable amour. And yet, I was unemployed.

Yup, despite my outward appearance, I was unemployed. I was told that I am expendable. Although I was considered an asset to the organization, it was not enough to maintain my position or salary in a cost-cutting organizational move that would ensure the shareholders realized their profit. Now, unfortunately, this happens to millions of people all the time. I wasn't the only individual let go. It wasn't a unique situation.

As I sat at the unemployment office trying to understand how I'd gotten here and what I'd done to deserve to be here, I quickly pivoted away from those thoughts and began to think instead, "*Why not me?*" I didn't know I was changing my mentality and how that would propel me to something better. No, that wasn't the thought at all. It was a simple question that I asked myself to consider all the things that had led to me sitting in this cold chair in this damp mildew-smelling room, waiting to be asked a bunch of questions by individuals that didn't care to be there.

As I asked myself that question, *"Why not me?"* I began to think about the person that was now my former boss and all the characteristics this individual displayed during this whole ordeal. I wanted to determine the lesson that I could have learned from this person to ensure I would never be in this position again. I thought about the few days that led up to this moment, where I would be sitting down with the *"executioner."* Yes, that may sound a bit hard, but that's what and how I thought of this person on that day in time. I've since had a change of heart.

You see, during the days leading up to it, my boss presented an air of confidence and security to the team. We discussed our work, our projects, our deadlines. We discussed the great things ahead and the impact we were going to make with our work. As you can imagine, these were all great signs of assurances that our jobs, and my job, in particular, were safe. Besides, there was no one else that could do what I do, right? *"Damn right,"* I told myself.

With all those assurances, I had prepared for our regularly scheduled one-on-one to update each other on our respective work. As the time neared and I prepared my presentation of deliverables, the *"executioner"* greeted me, followed by a quickly scurrying boss that left the call as if he were Usain Bolt setting a new 100-meter world record. I mean this guy couldn't get out of there fast enough. No eye contact, no greeting, no "f-u".. *"Hard times call for tough decisions"* is what I remember as I became cold and distant from the conversation that was about to take place. There was absolutely no humanity in that experience or dialogue, only survival!

As the call with the *"executioner"* ended, I gathered my thoughts, grabbed my things, and walked down the *"hall of shame"* as some had called it. The only thing that I couldn't wrap my head around was that the feeling that I had wasn't exactly one filled with rage, anger, sadness, or worry. Sure, those feelings eventually crept in, but while I was making that dramatic walk, stuff in hand, those feelings were nowhere to be found.

I was still sitting in this cold, navy blue plastic chair with no armrest, trying to find some semblance of comfort. People were coughing, sneezing, crying, talking loudly to each other, or pacing back and forth. I just sat there. I had my carrier bag with me. I usually had this bag with me, and in it, I had a notebook. I had no idea how much longer I would be sitting there, so I pulled out the notebook, and I began to write.

The journey of writing sometimes has no particular destination. That's what makes it an adventure. As I put pen to pad, I found myself wandering through all types of uncharted territories. I saw signs along the way that guided other thoughts and pushed me to go down different paths in my writing. I found adventure, chaos, and treasure. Writing became a sort of therapy in what should have been a turbulent time. It became the moments of reflection that I needed. It became my refuge. In my writing expeditions, I discovered that this experience that had me sitting in this brightly-lit, windowless office space with the hard blue plastic chairs should be an opportunity to teach myself and others valuable lessons learned when blessed with disappointment. I kept writing.

A man in brown pants, black hard bottom patent-leather shoes, a checkered pattern button-down shirt, and a blue cross-stitched tie shouted, "*Se-en Bailey.*" Again, "*Se-en Bailey.*" I responded, "Do you mean *Sean Bailey?*" His response: "*Yeah, sure. Come this way.*" He began to ask me a few questions, and I stopped him and asked him, "*What does this job teach you about people, about yourself?*" He looked at me, paused, and said in reply, "*I don't understand what you mean.*"

I knew then that this is what I wanted and needed to do. I needed to help people learn about themselves so that they could learn for themselves. I left before the interview was over because I realized that my journey had given me another sign. Life had been listening to me. I never looked back.

Sean "Bear" Bailey
Credit image: Bear and Bailey Productions

Dr. Sean Bailey is a highly respected senior researcher, trainer, leadership coach, author and keynote speaker. He is the President of BCG Learning Solutions, an Education Technology and Workforce Development Training company. He is also the Bailey Institute for Research and Development Chairman, a nonprofit, public research institute bridging the gap between learning research and practical application.

For the past 20 years, he has specialized in continuous improvement working with Educational Institutions, local and state governmental entities, Healthcare organizations, and manufacturing companies. He often speaks about self-management and improving personal systems to help develop productive habits and a growth mindset.

Dr. Bailey is certified as a Professional in Learning and Performance, as well as, certified in Neuro-Linguistic Programming. Dr. Bailey holds a Doctorate in Educational Leadership from Creighton University. He completed his Executive MBA from the University of Maryland, College Park and Masters in Public Administration with an emphasis in Public Service.

He adores his family, his animals, live music, outdoor adventures, the ocean, street tacos, and most importantly, being present in the moment. When asked about his attitude towards life, his response is simple, "It's magical."